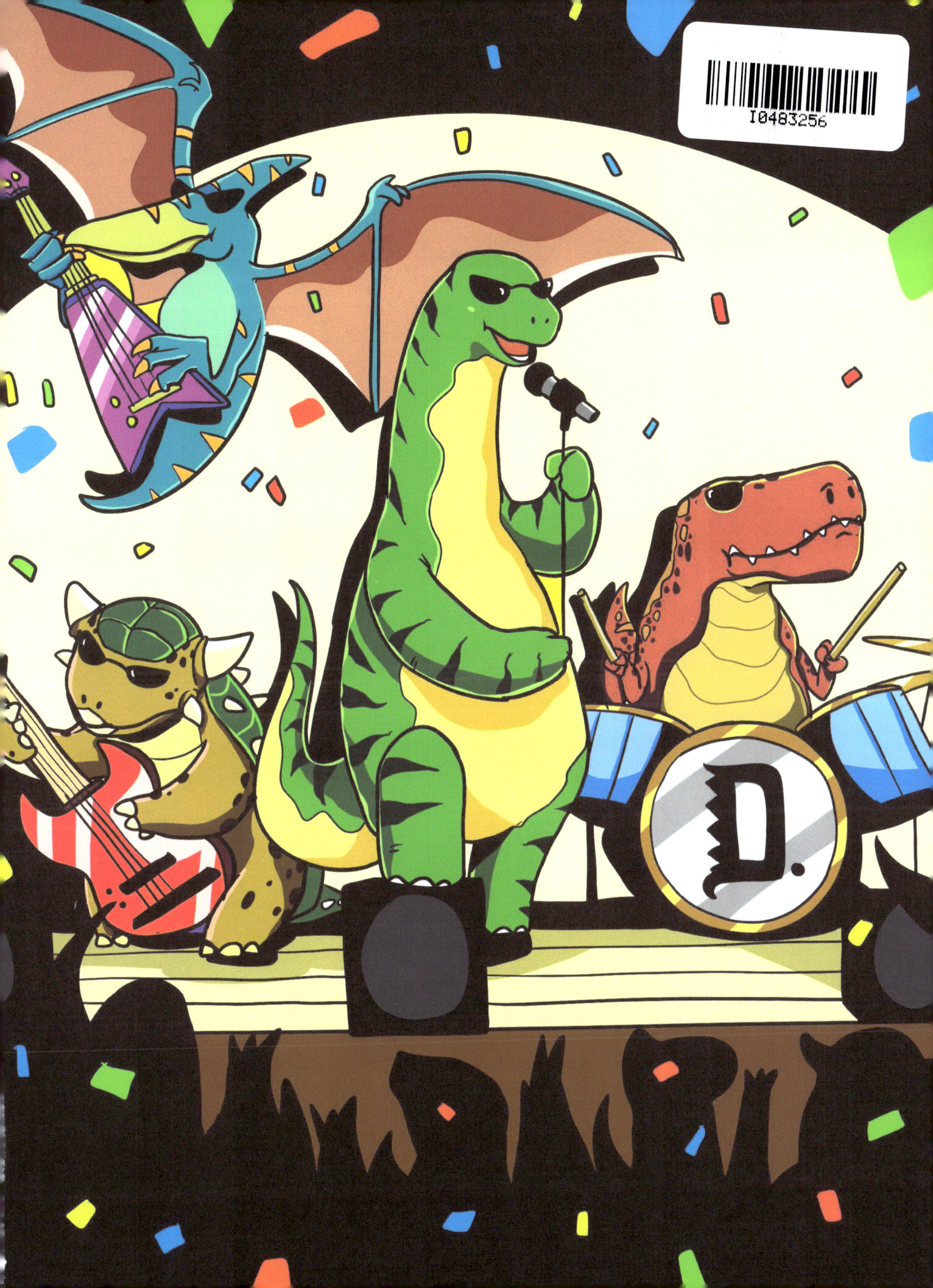

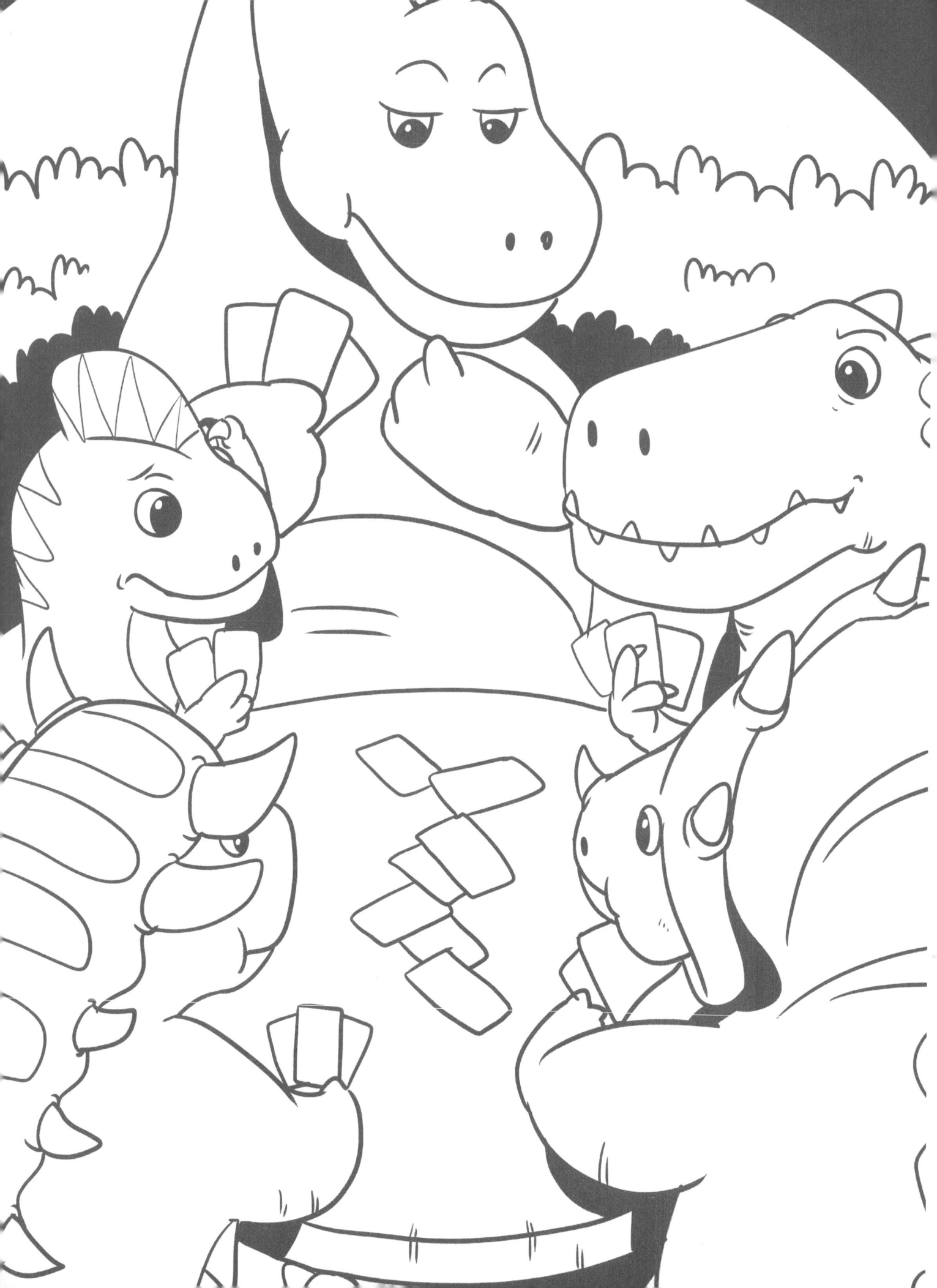

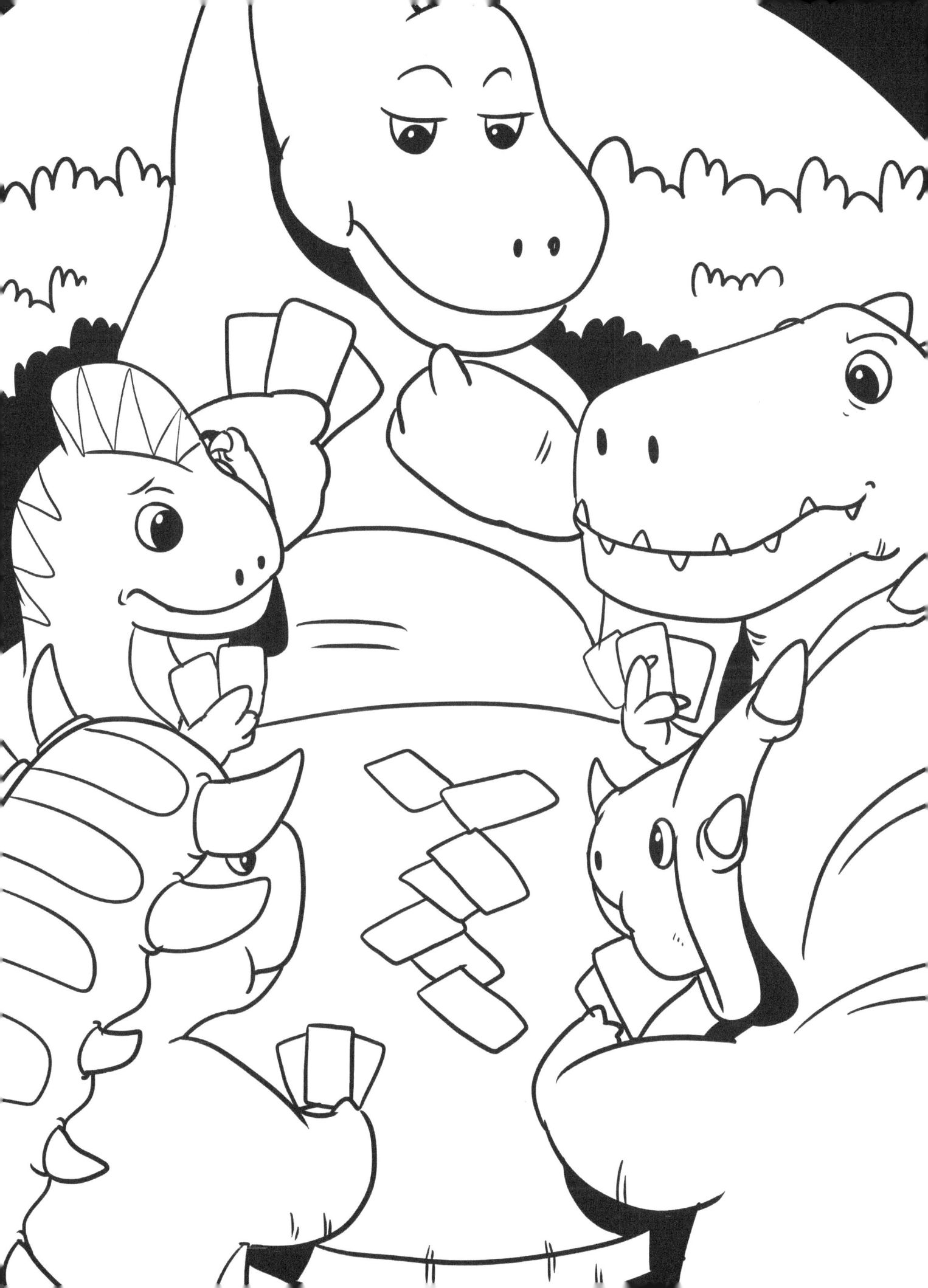

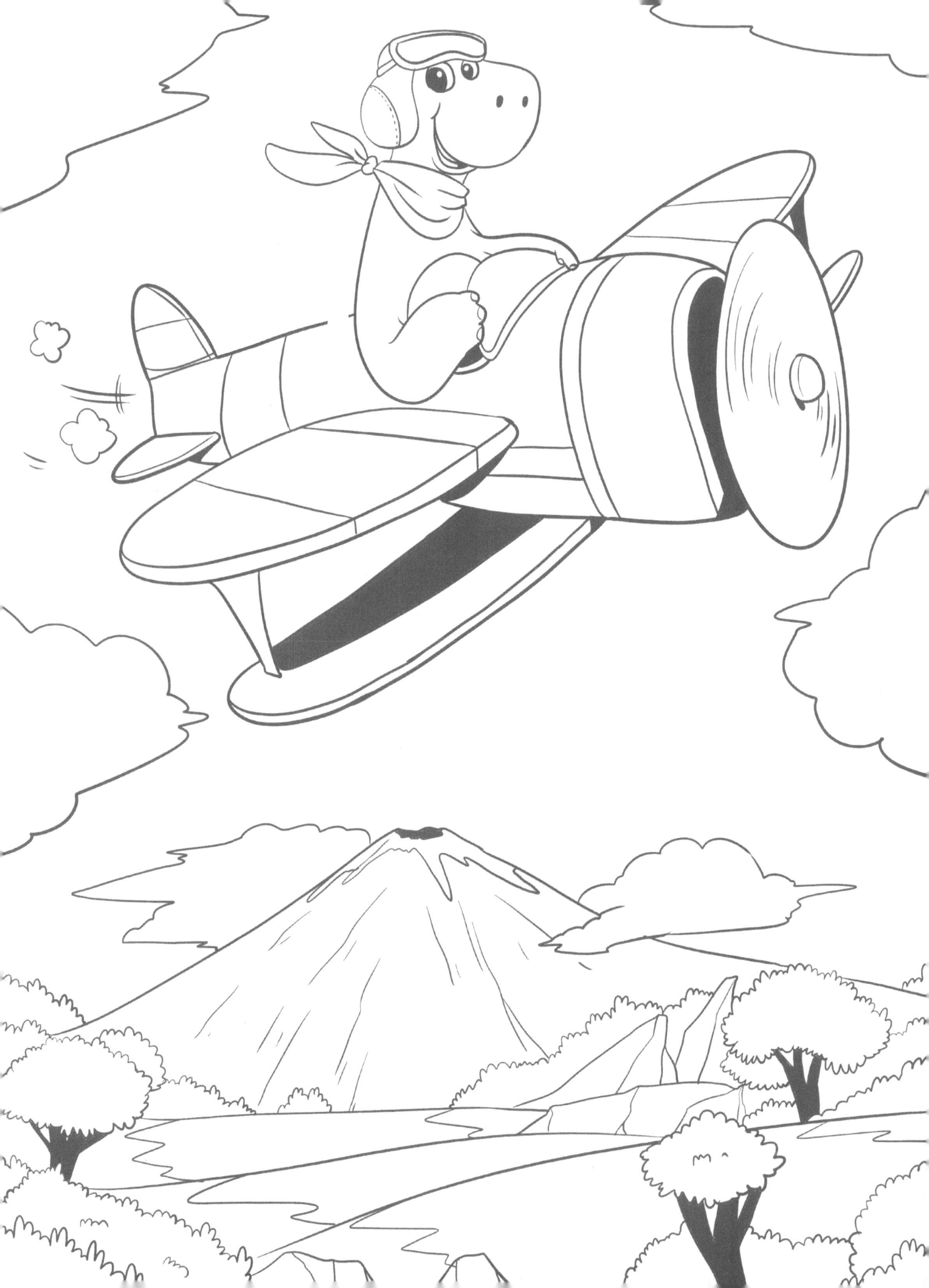

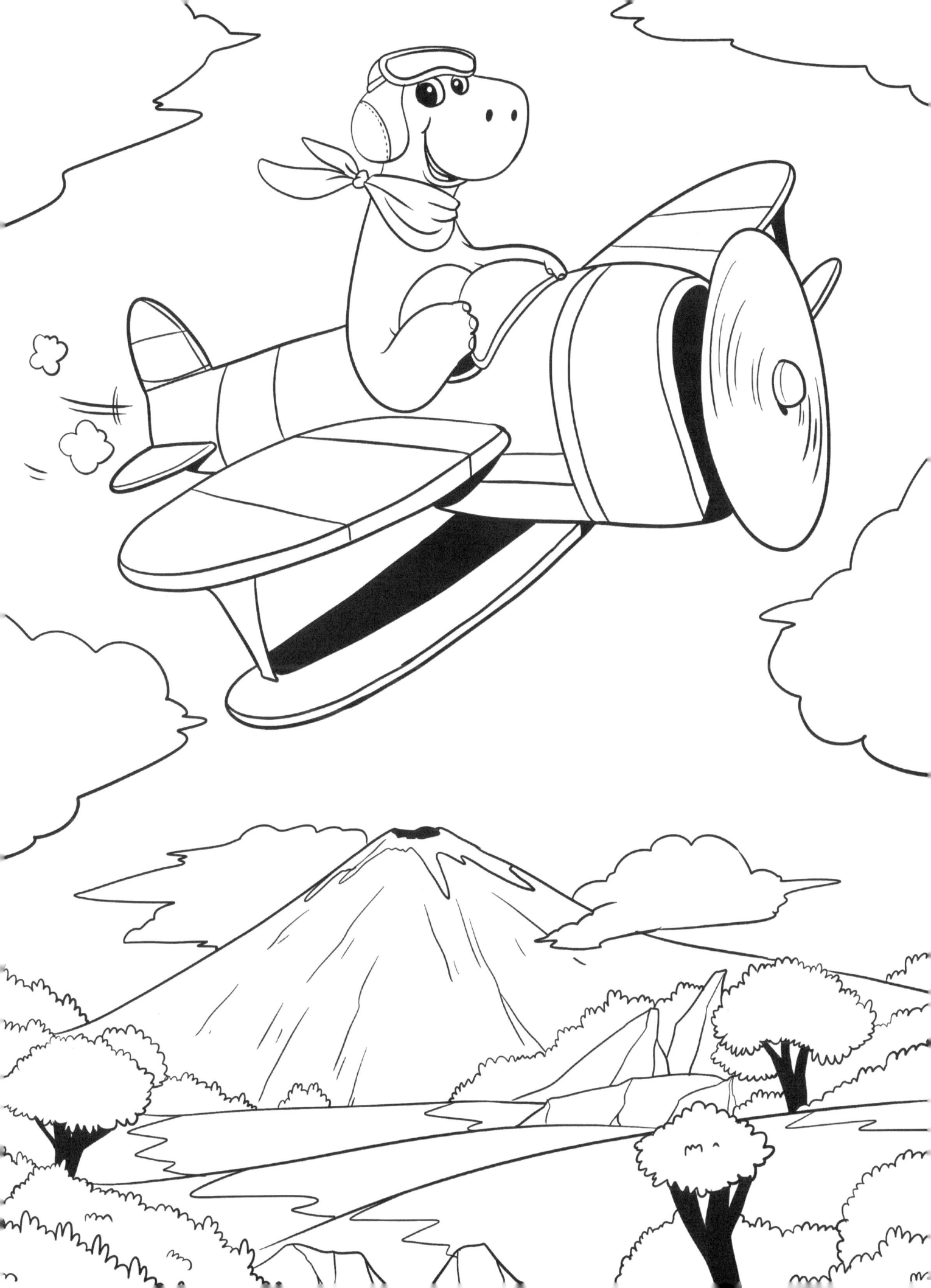

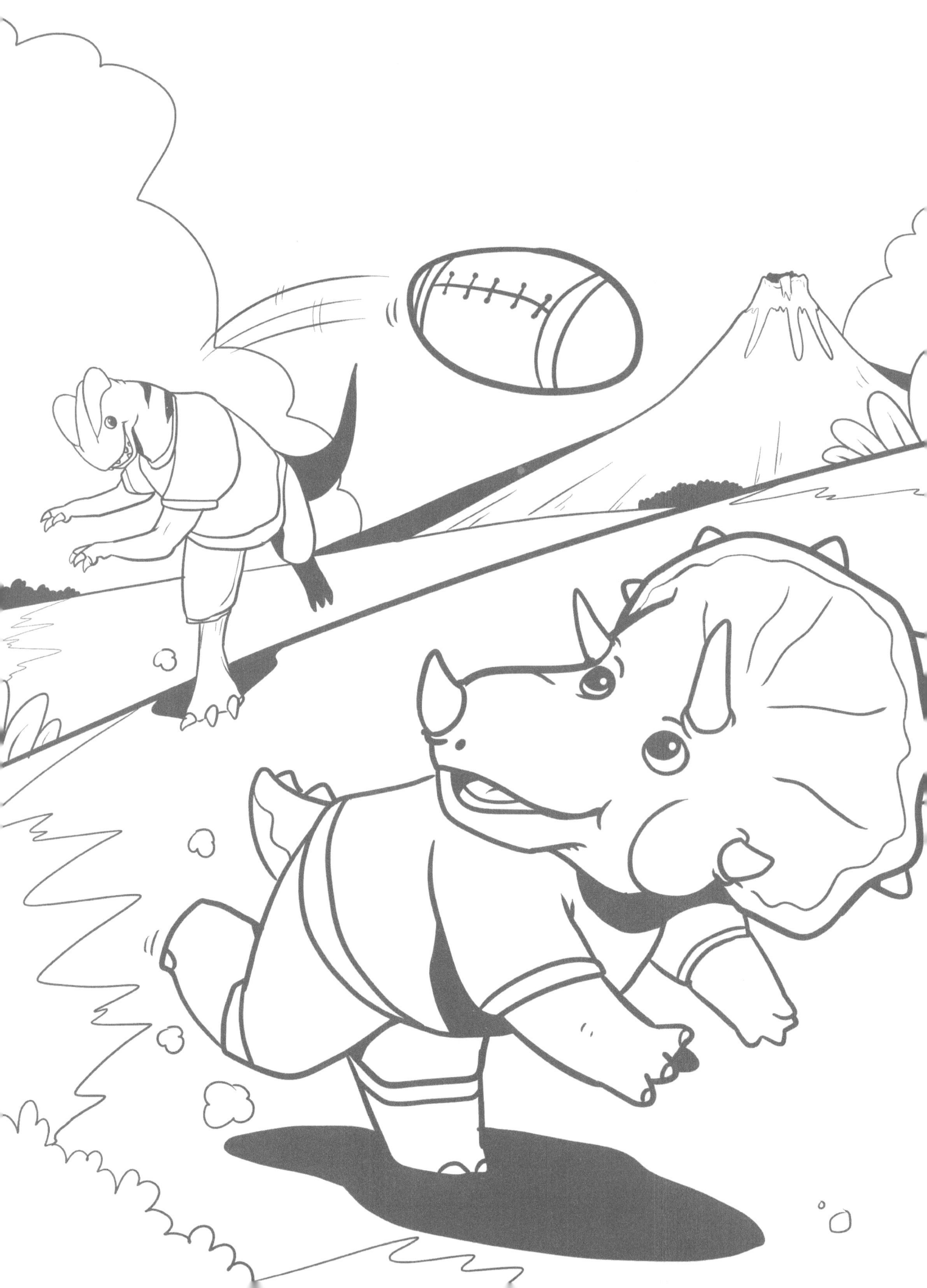

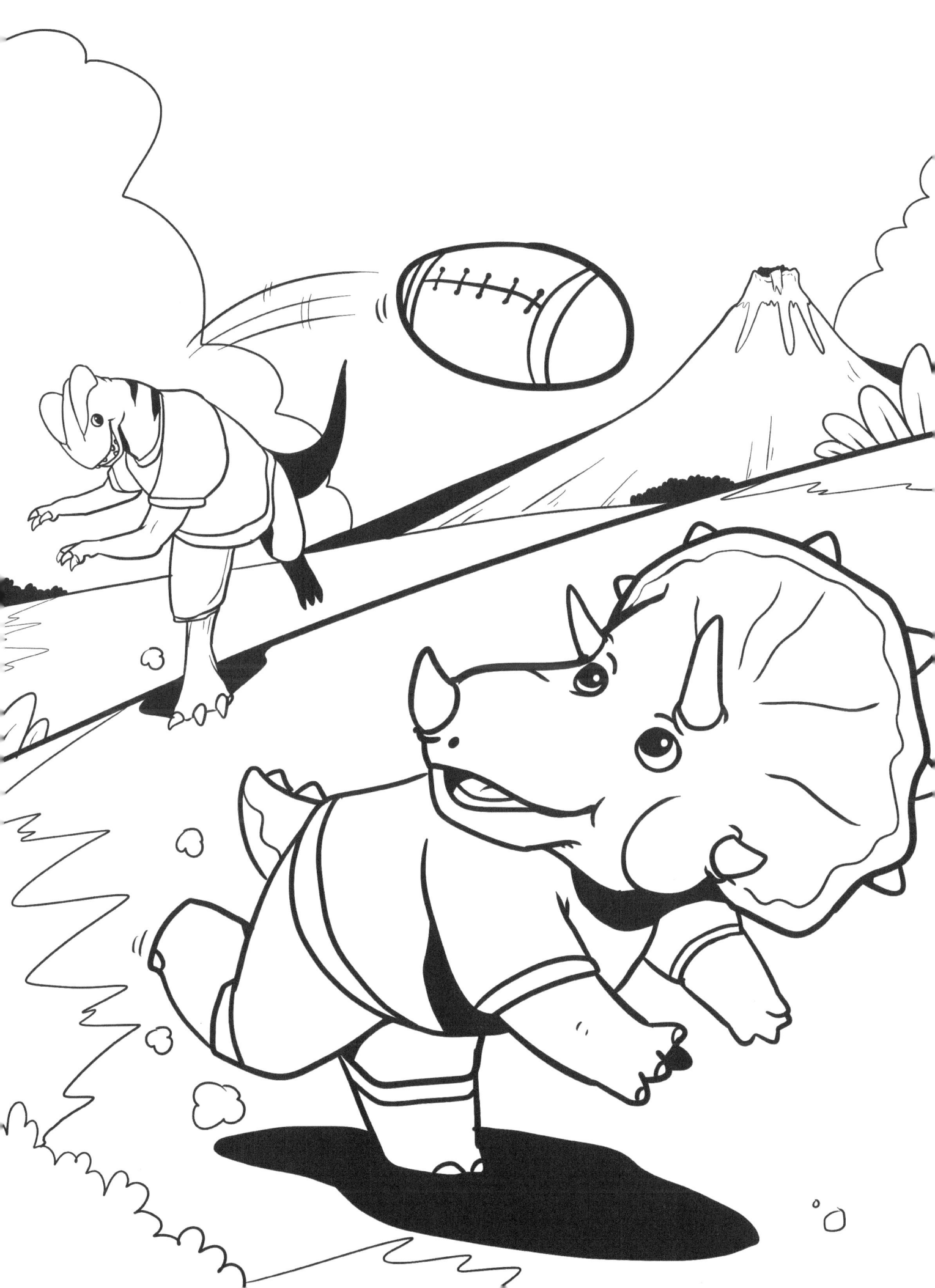

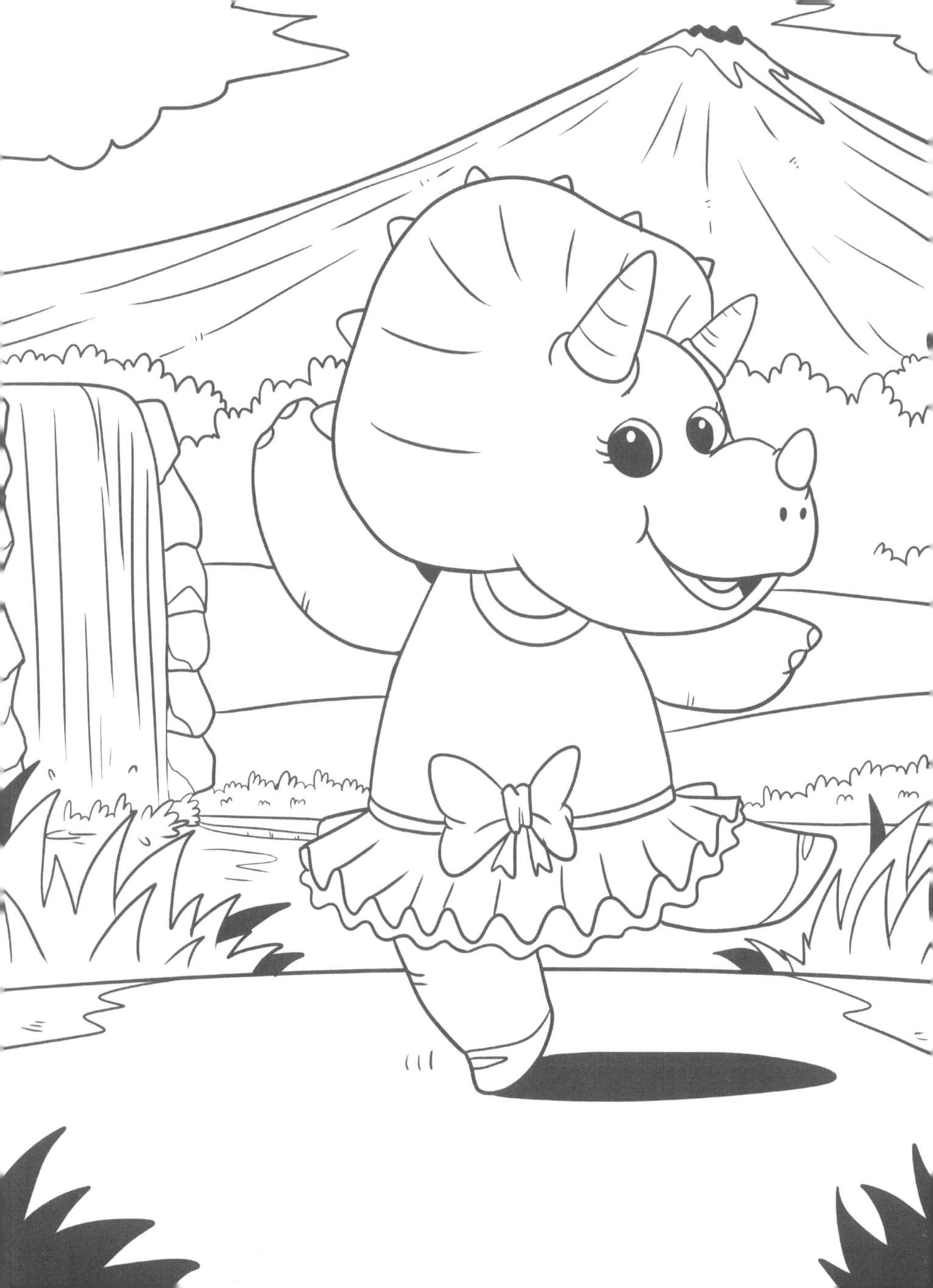

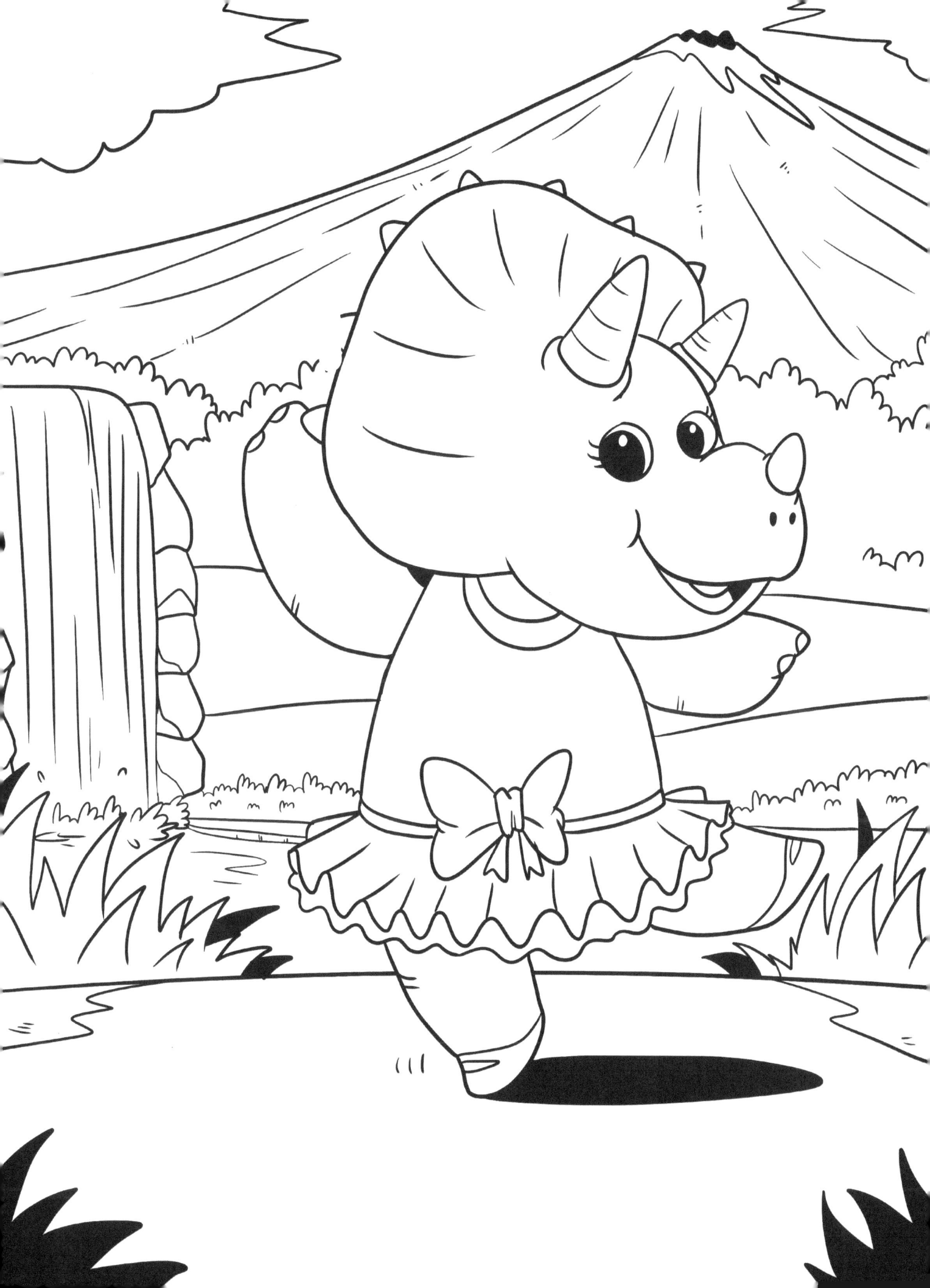

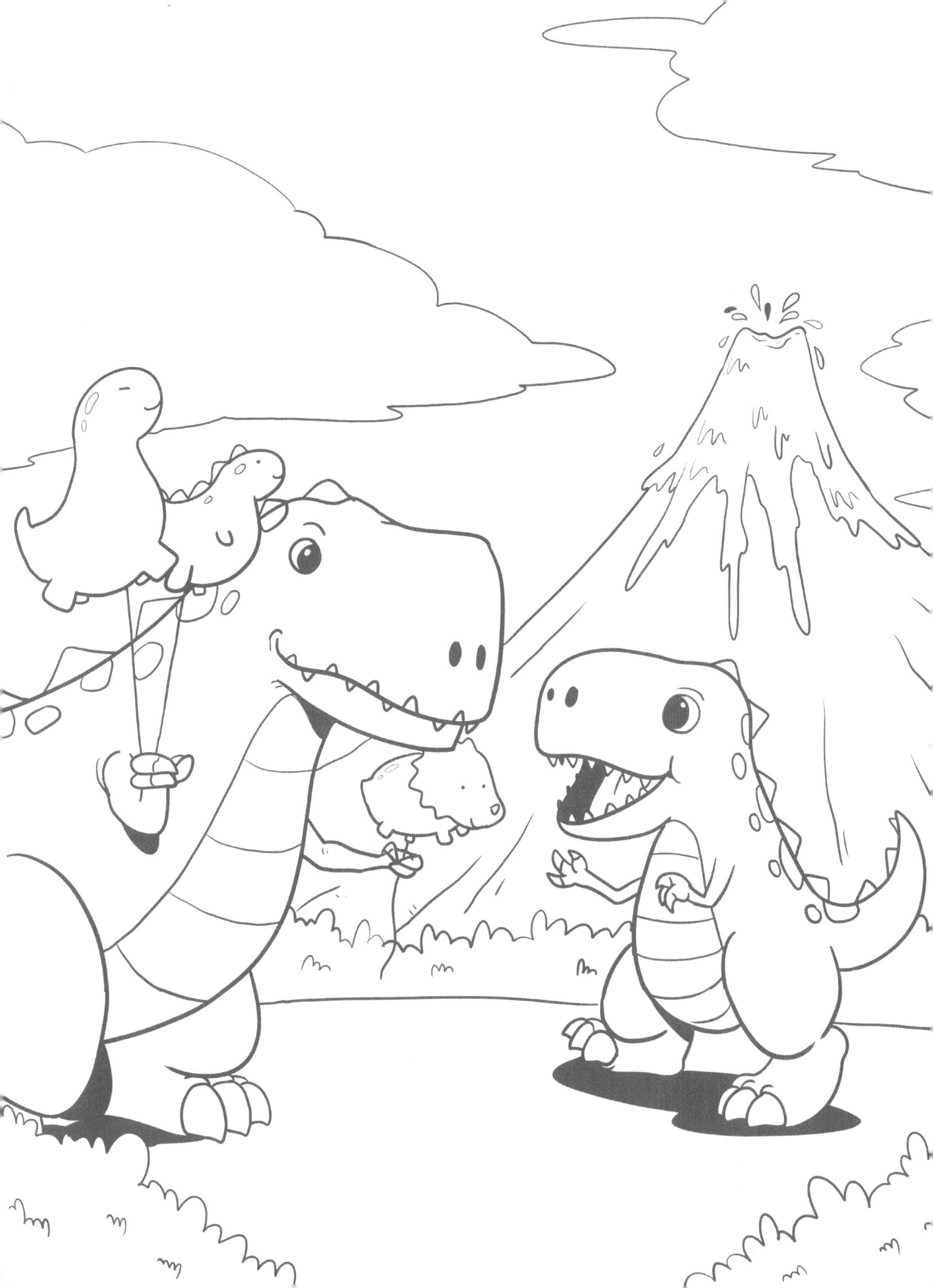

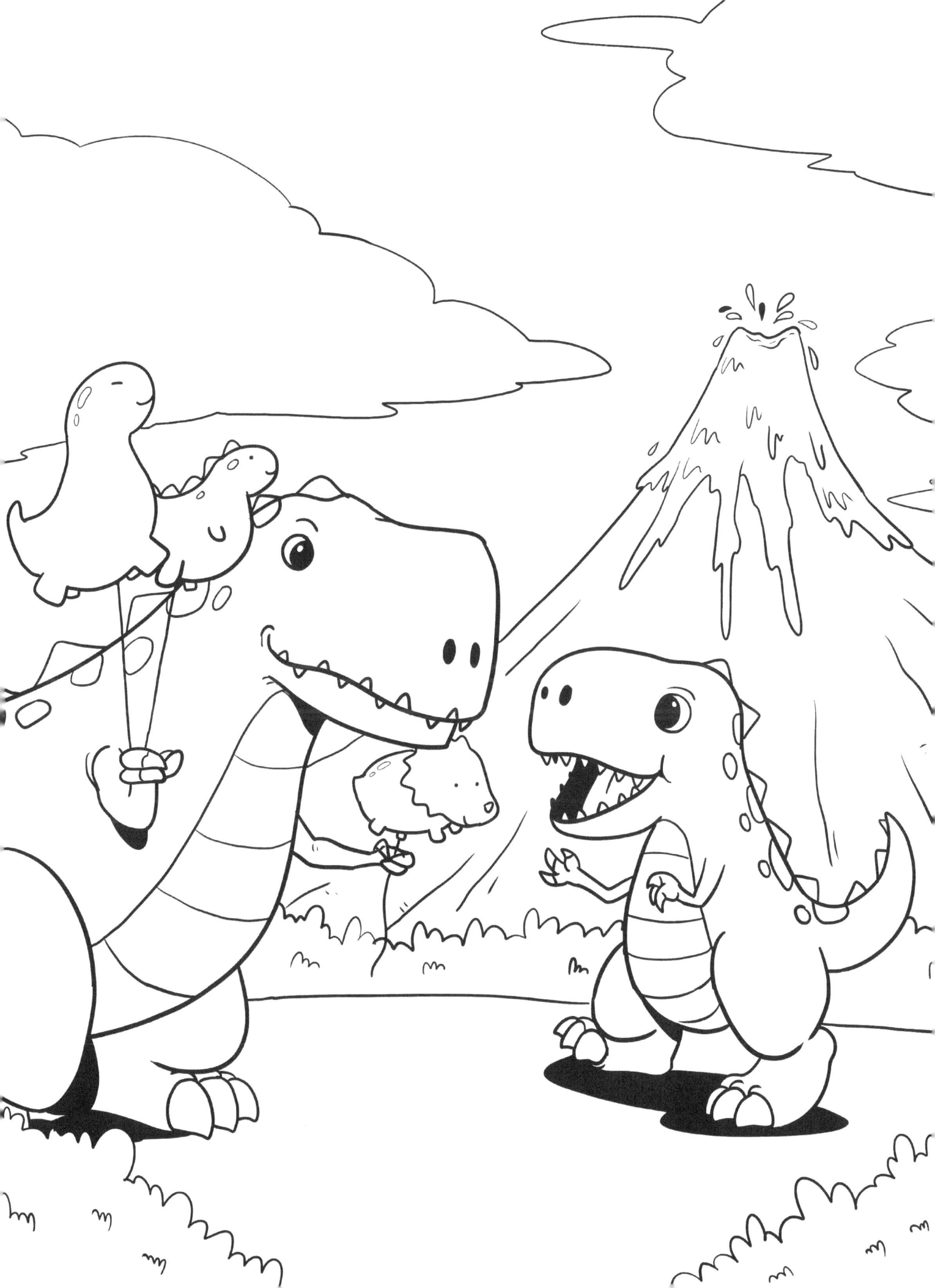

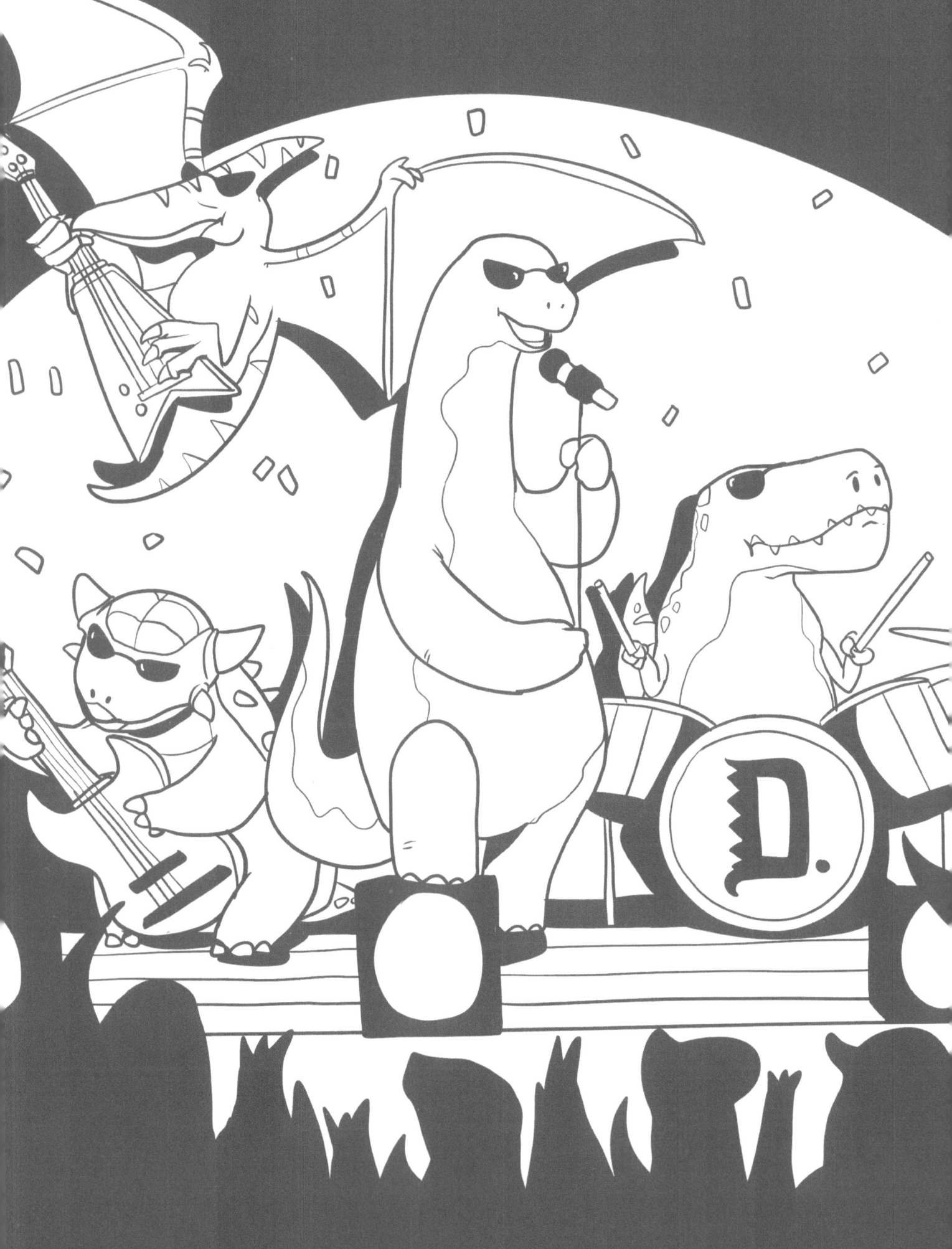

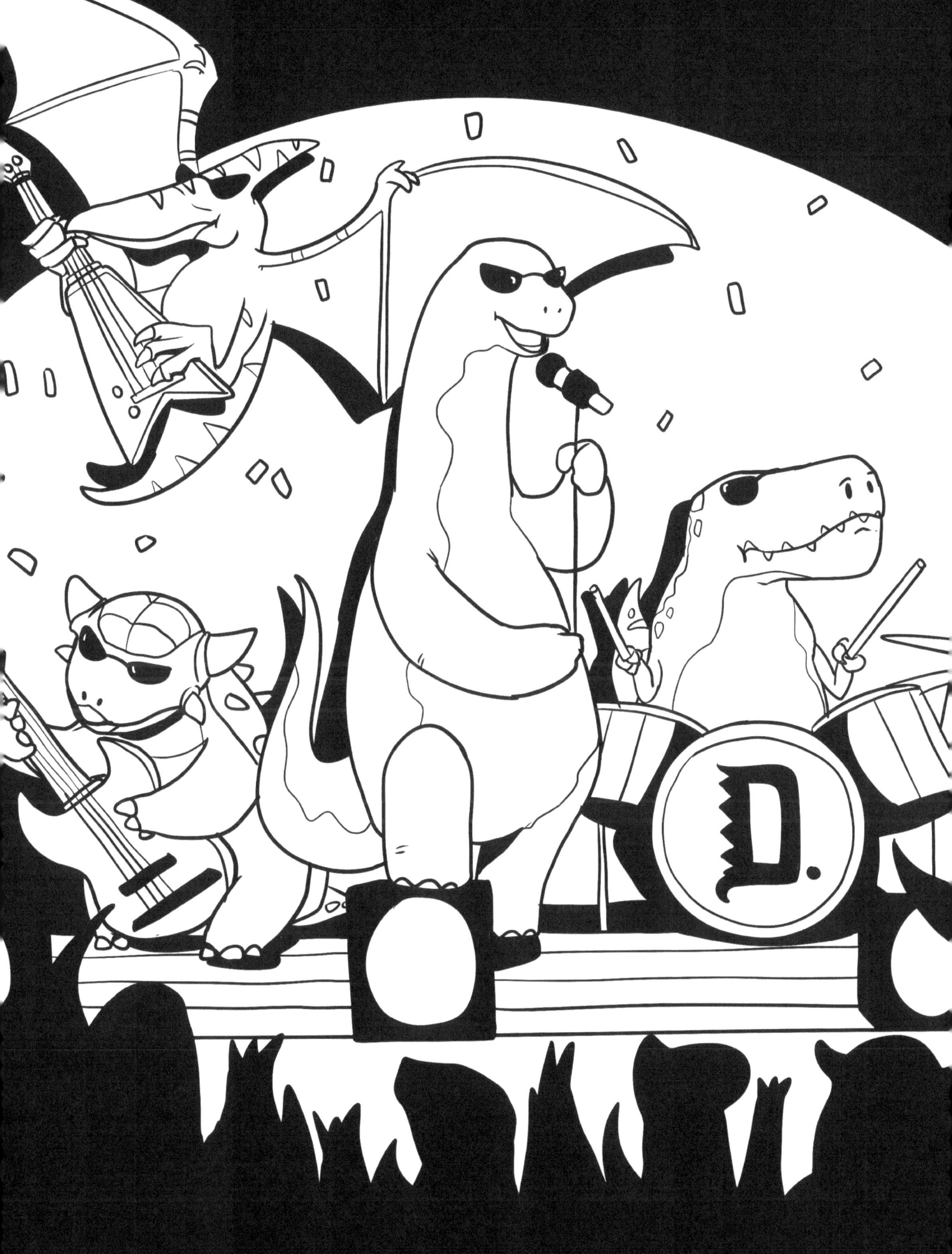

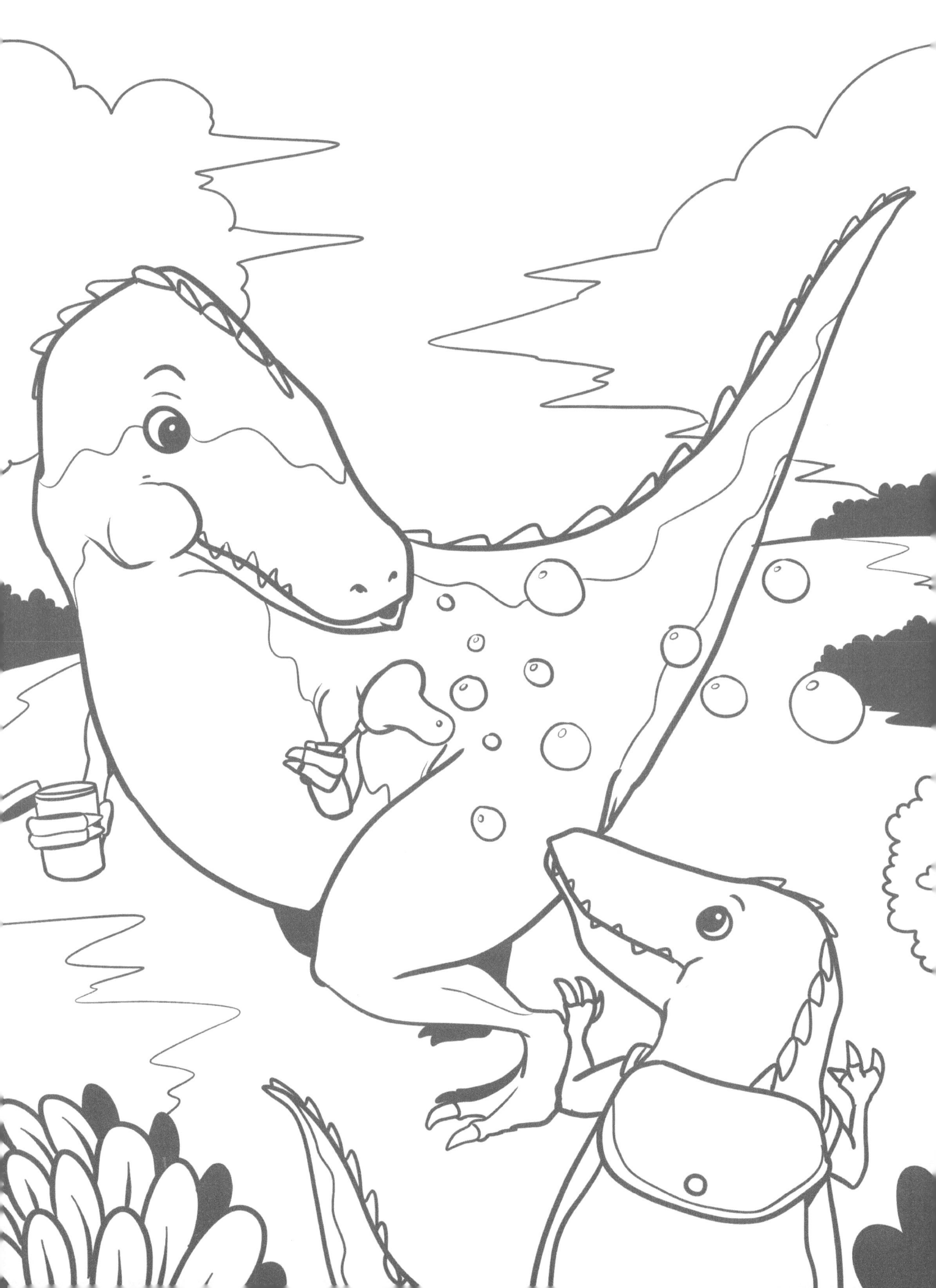

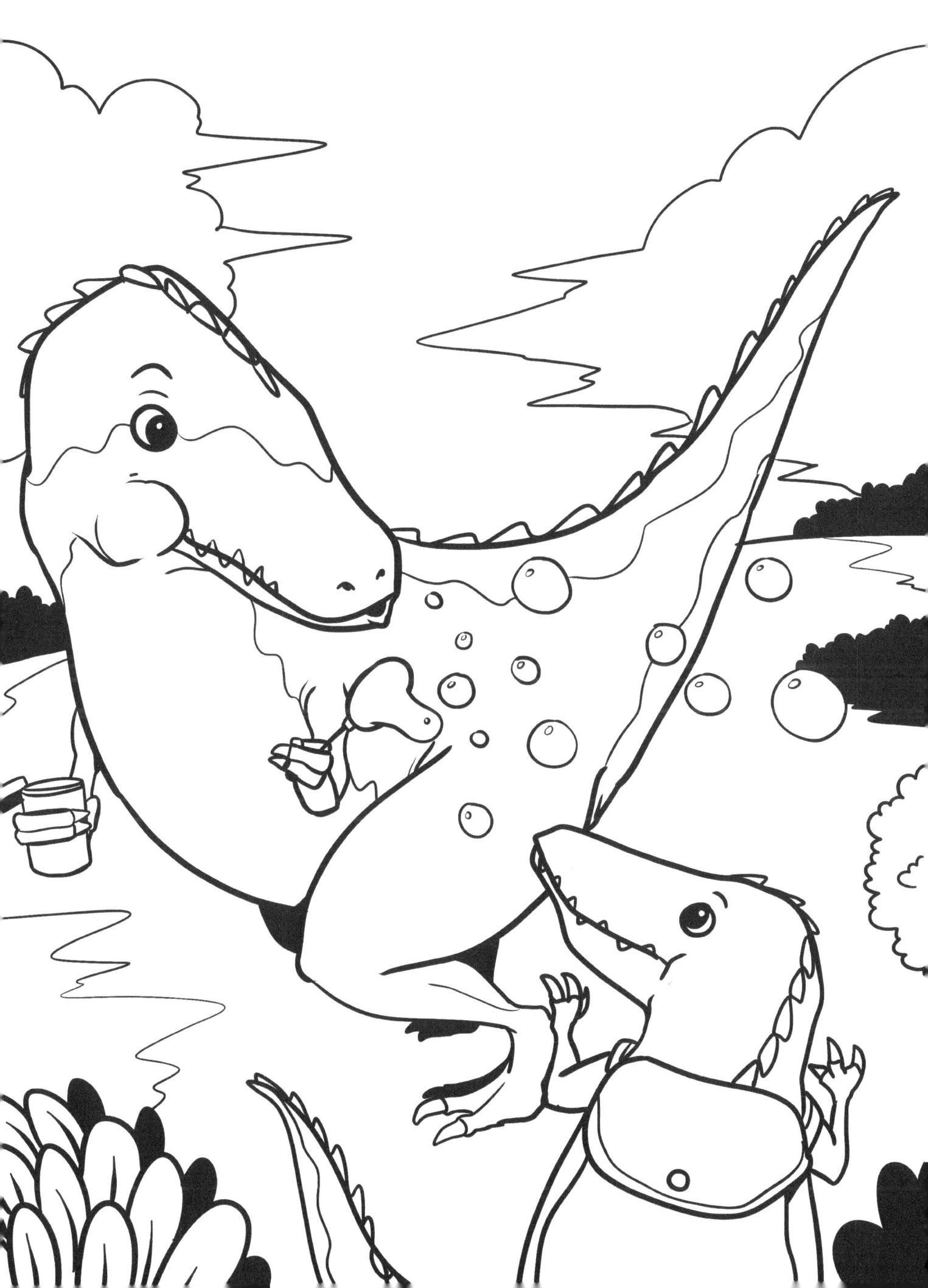

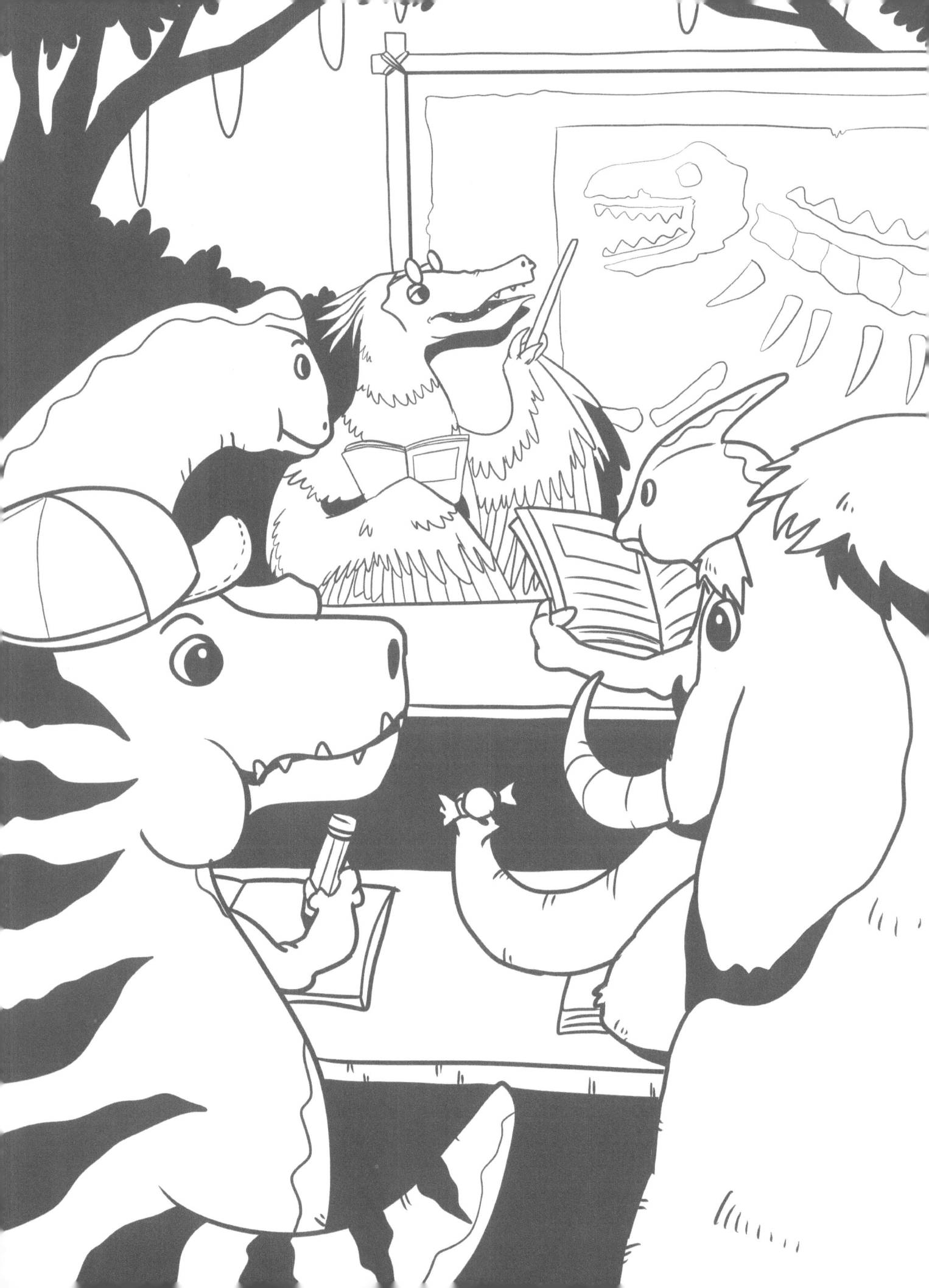

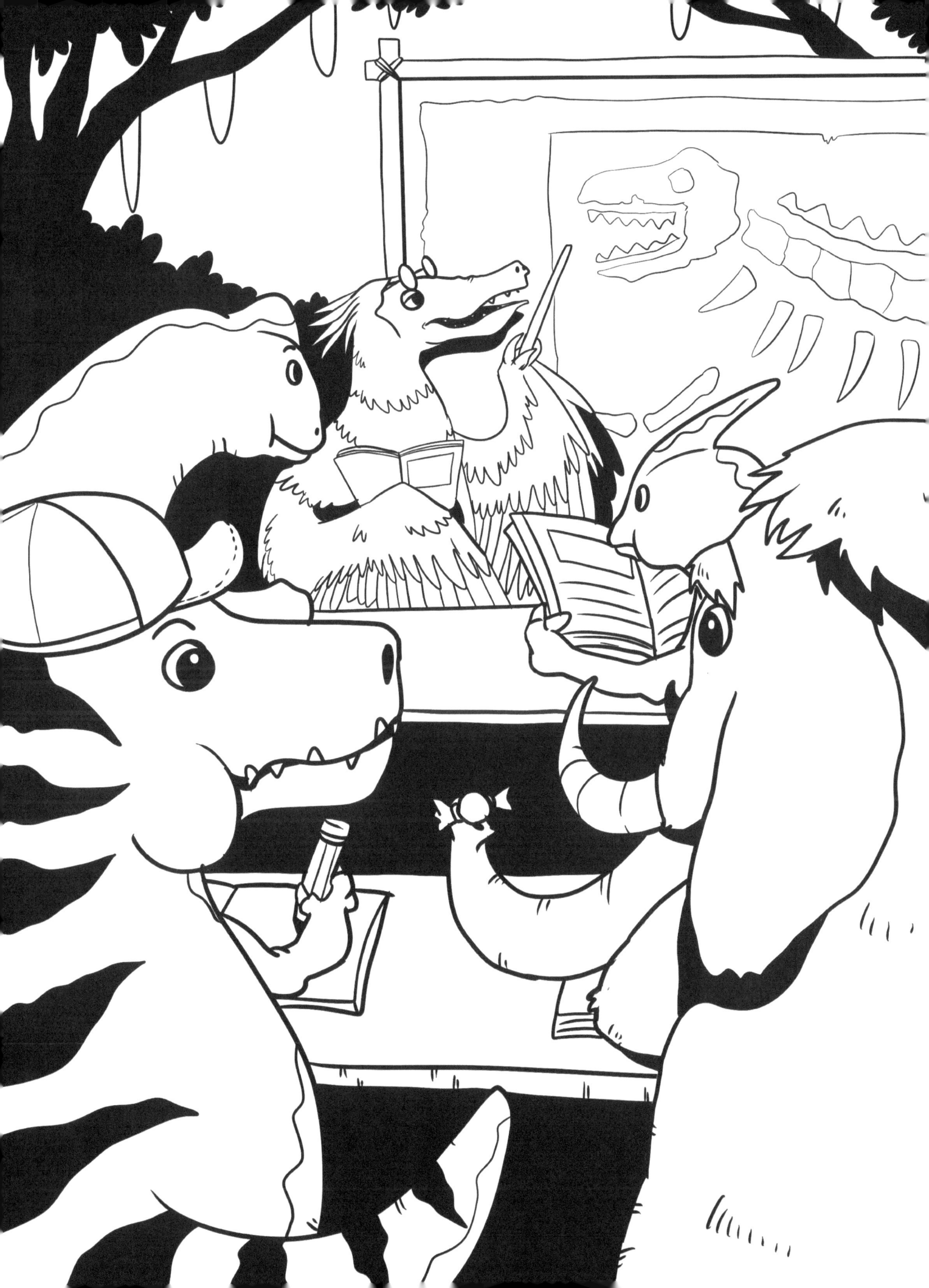

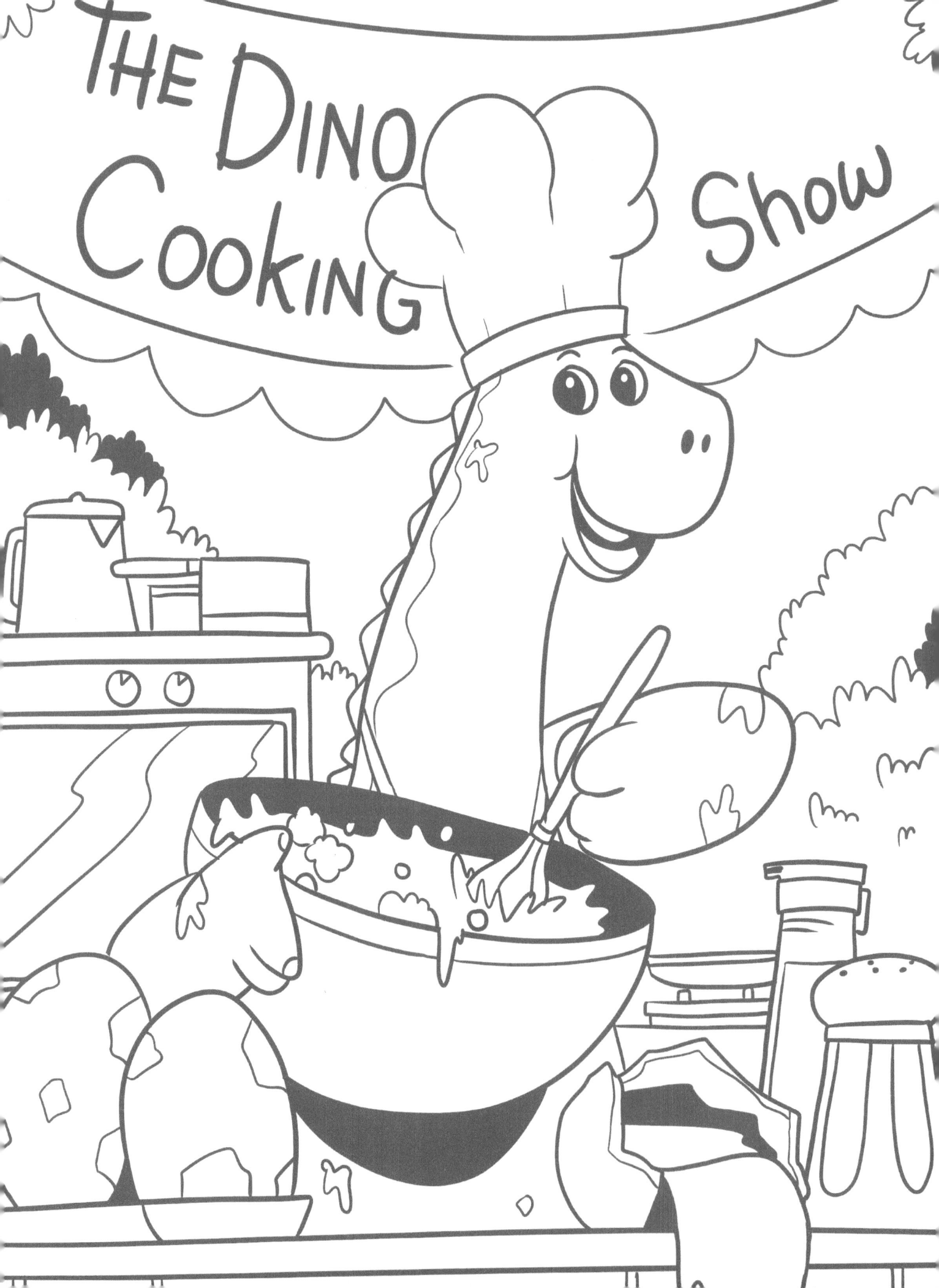

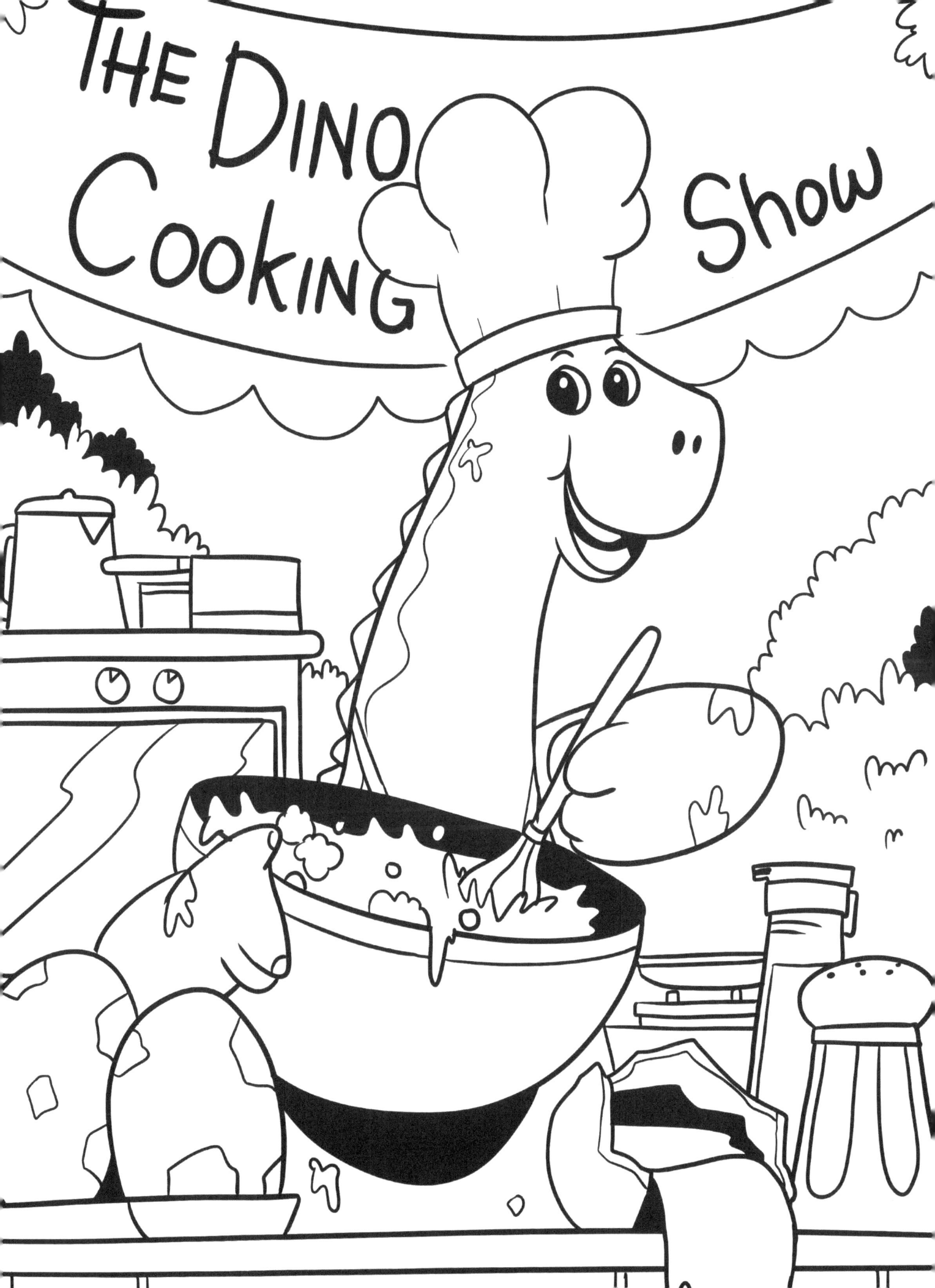

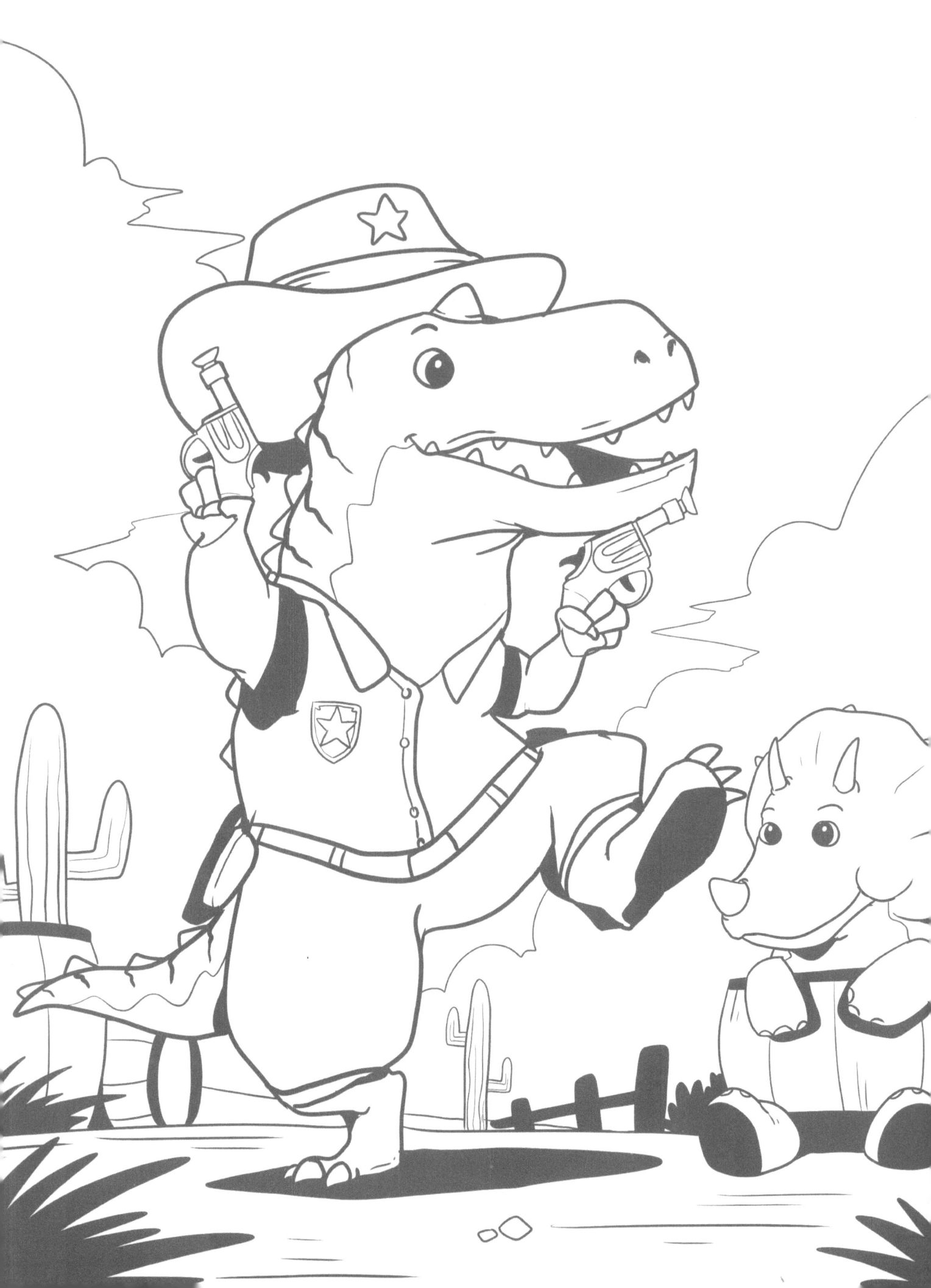

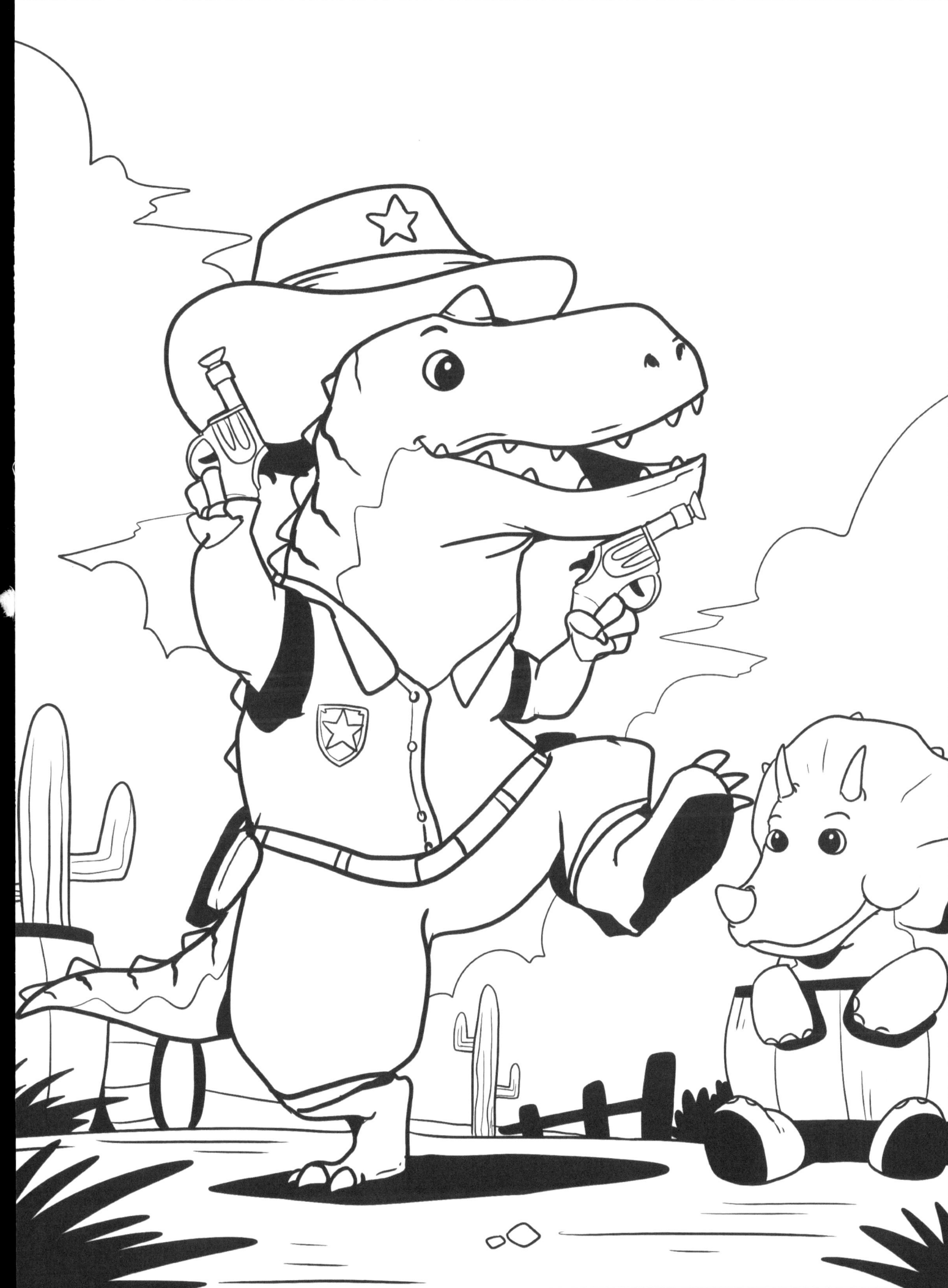

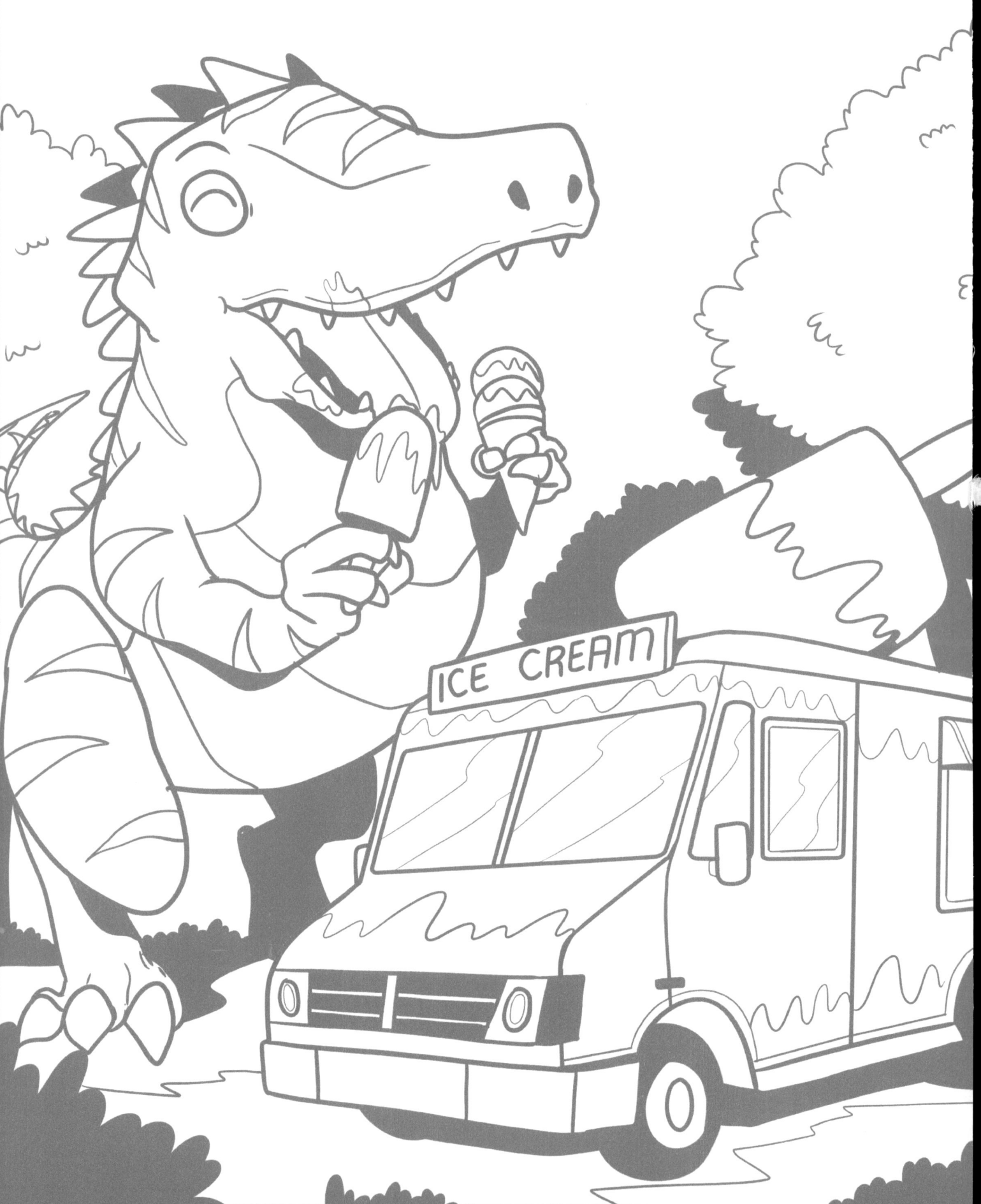

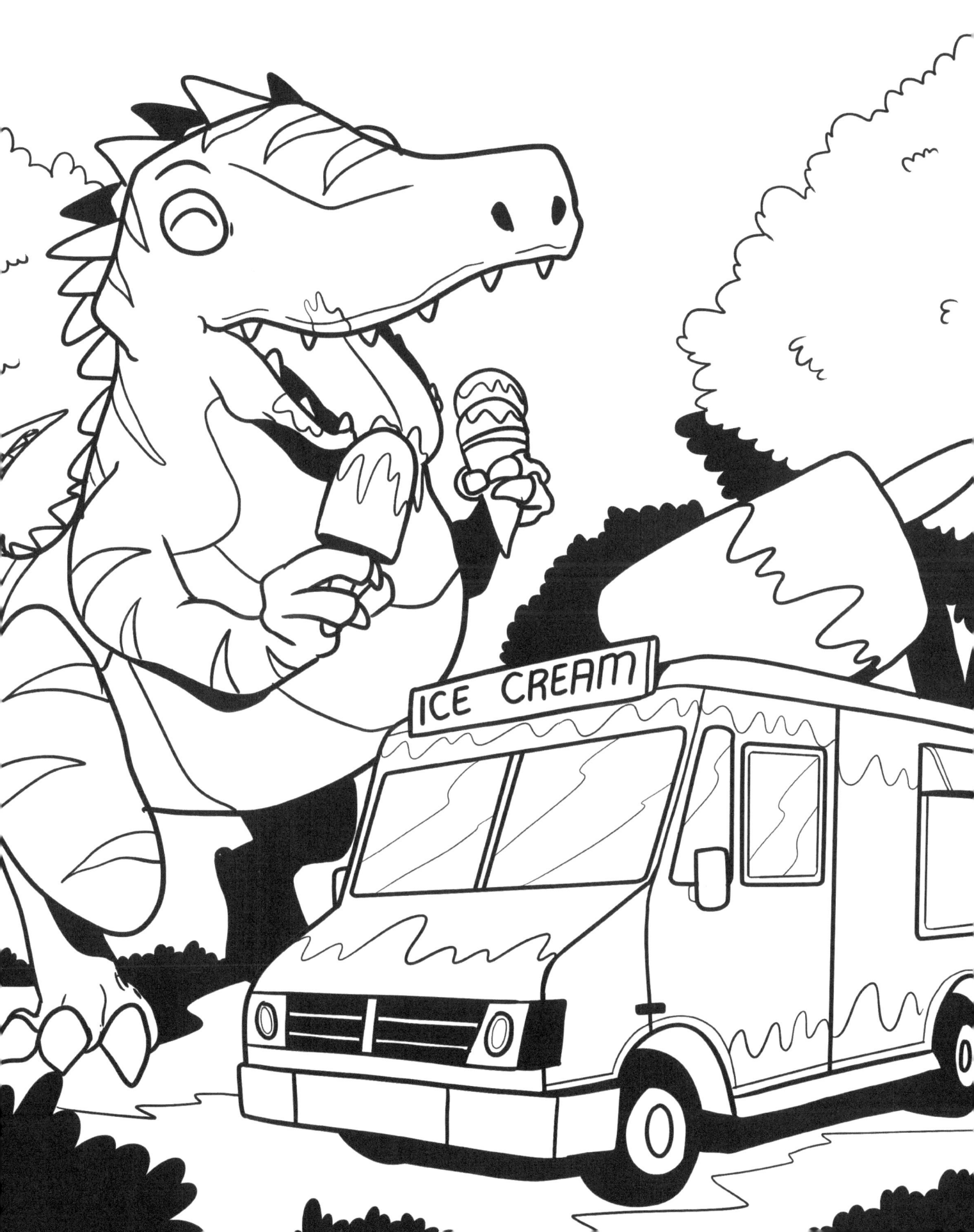

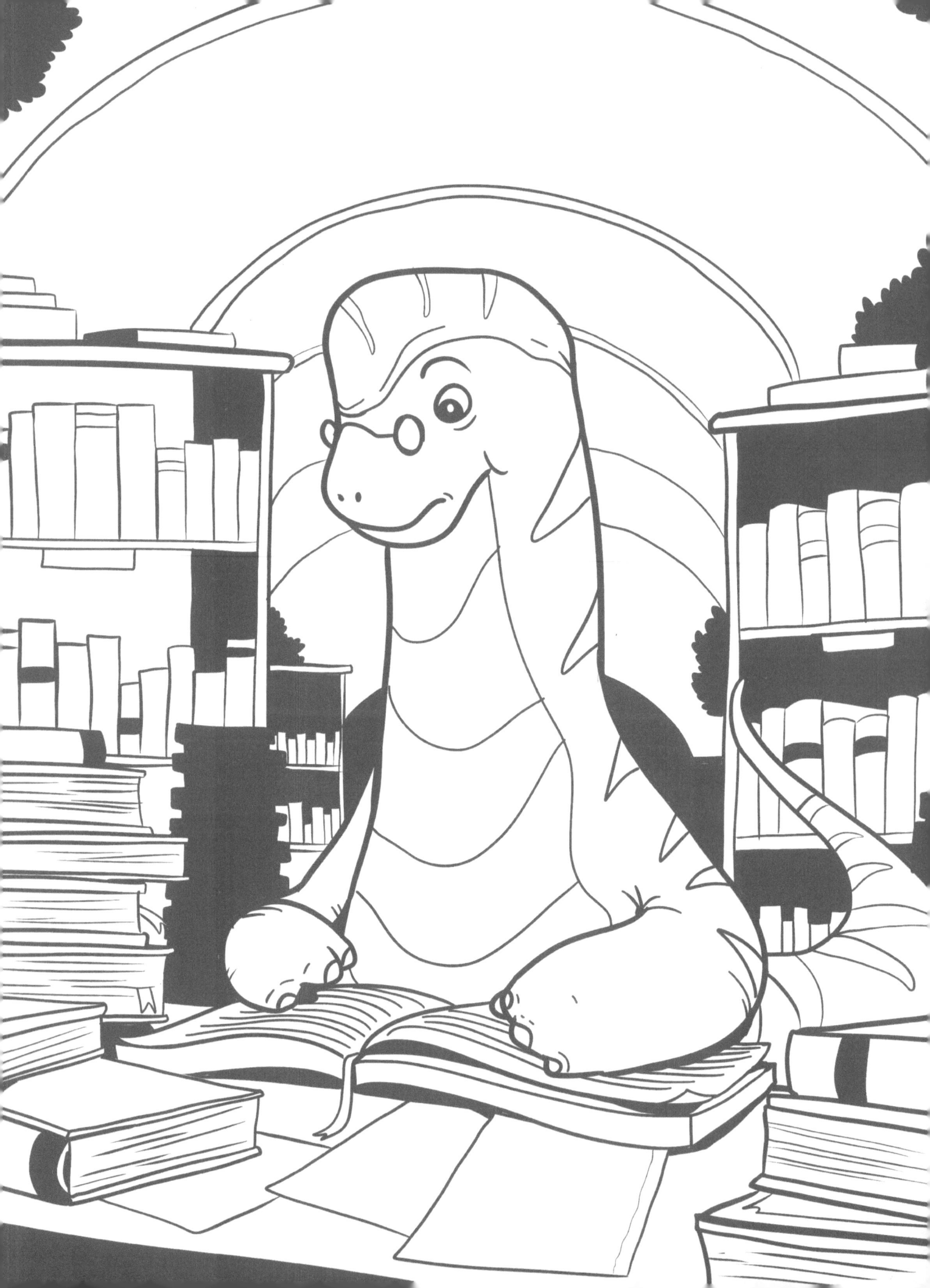

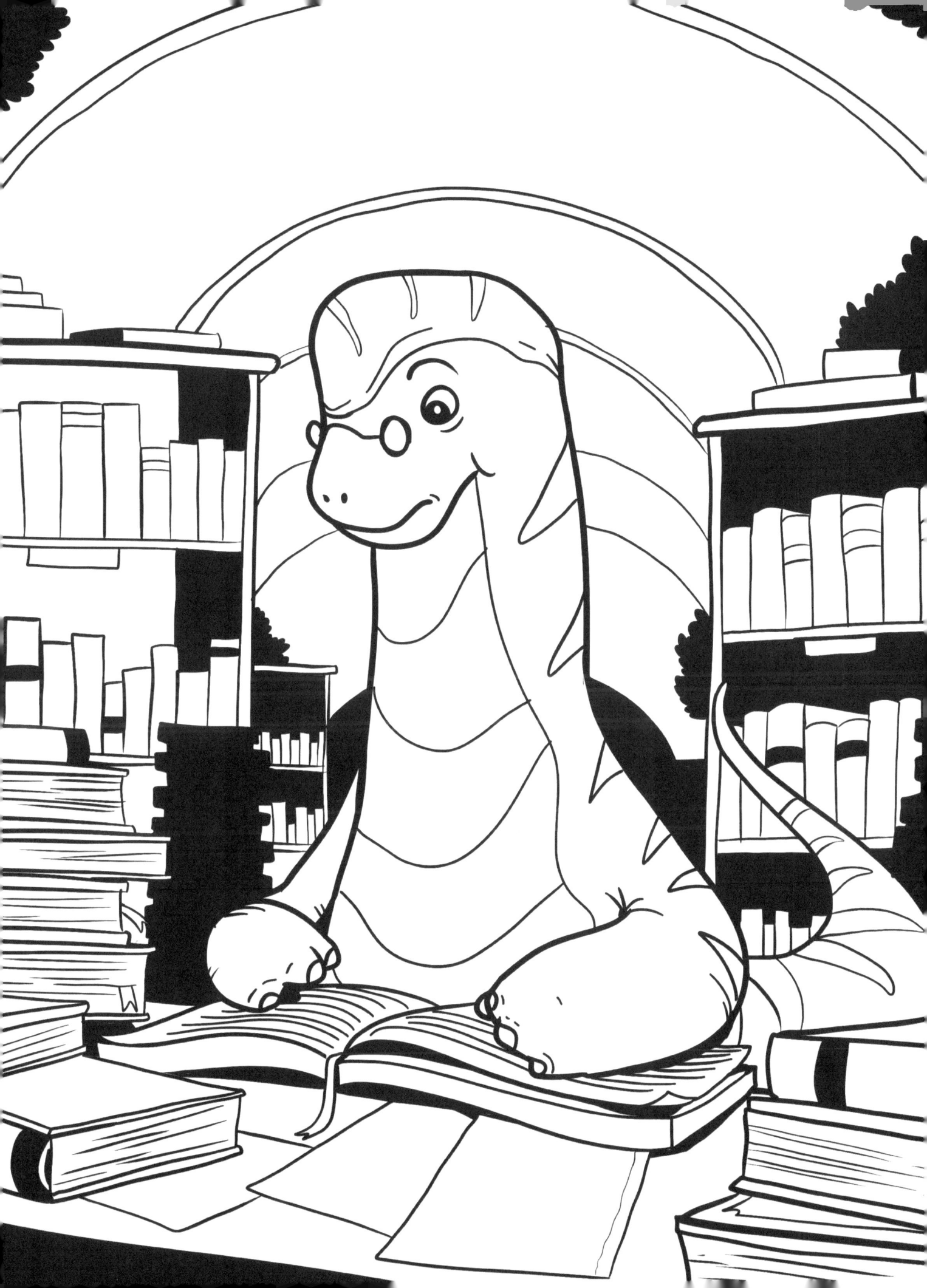

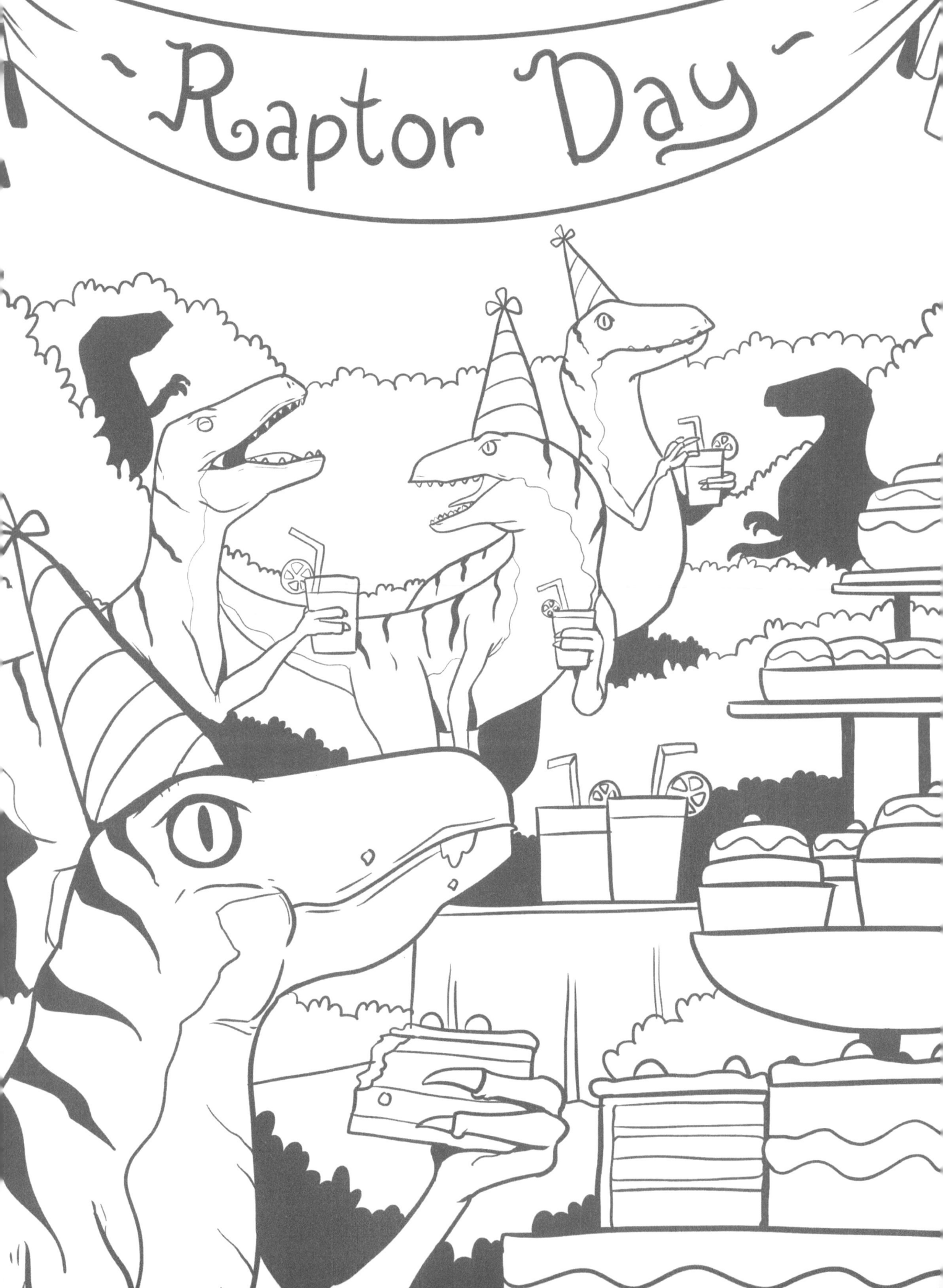

Raptor Day

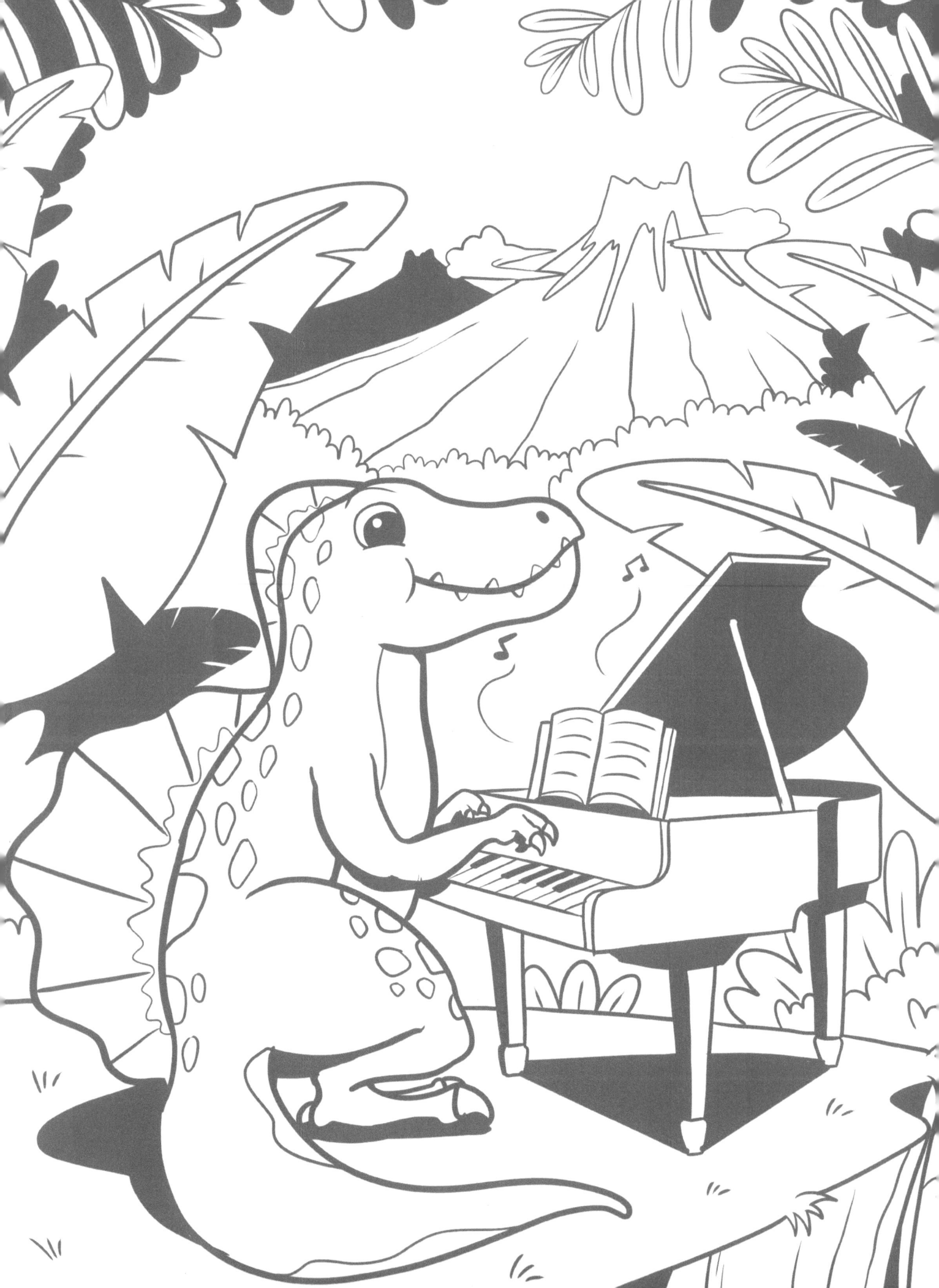

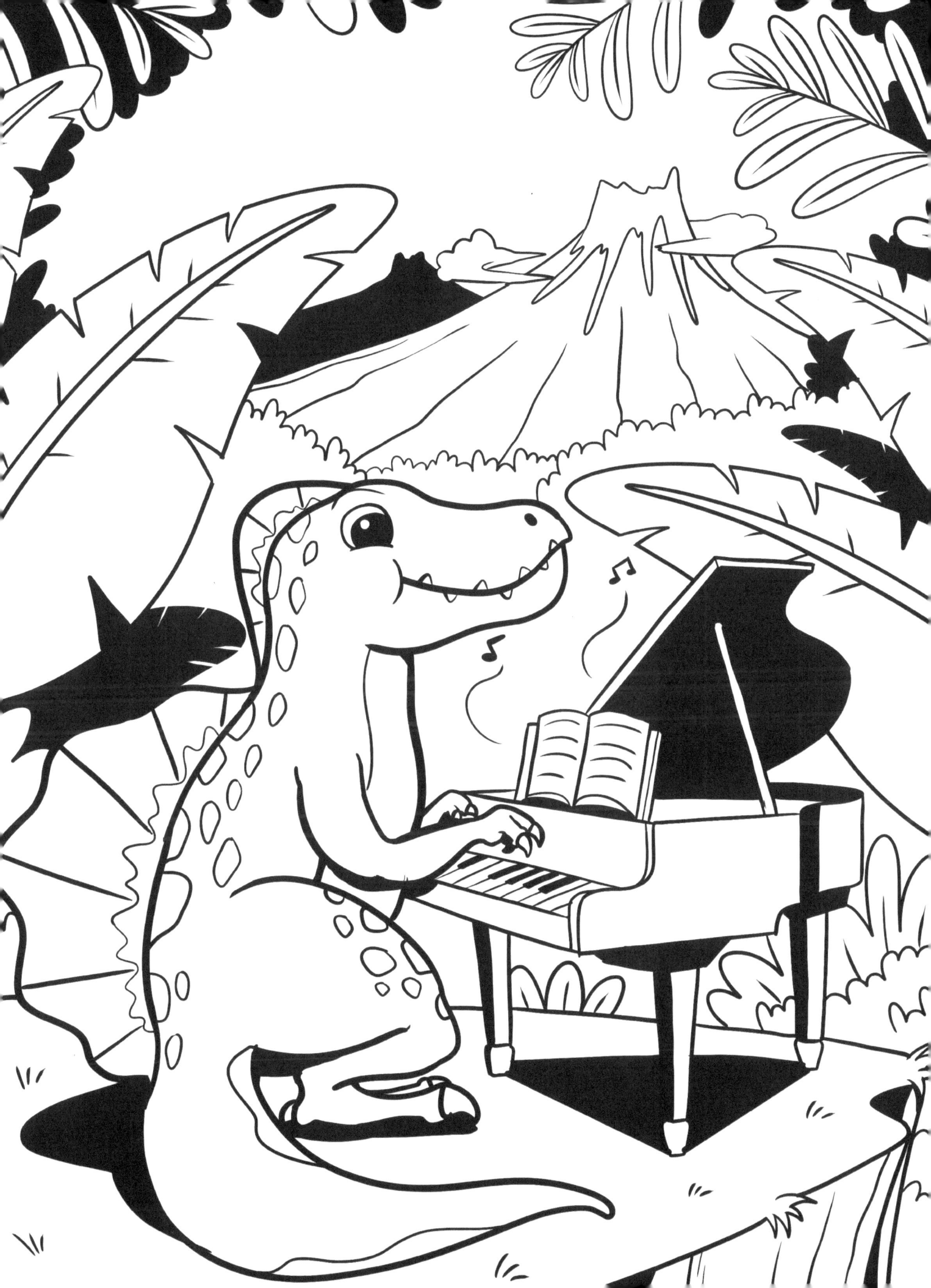

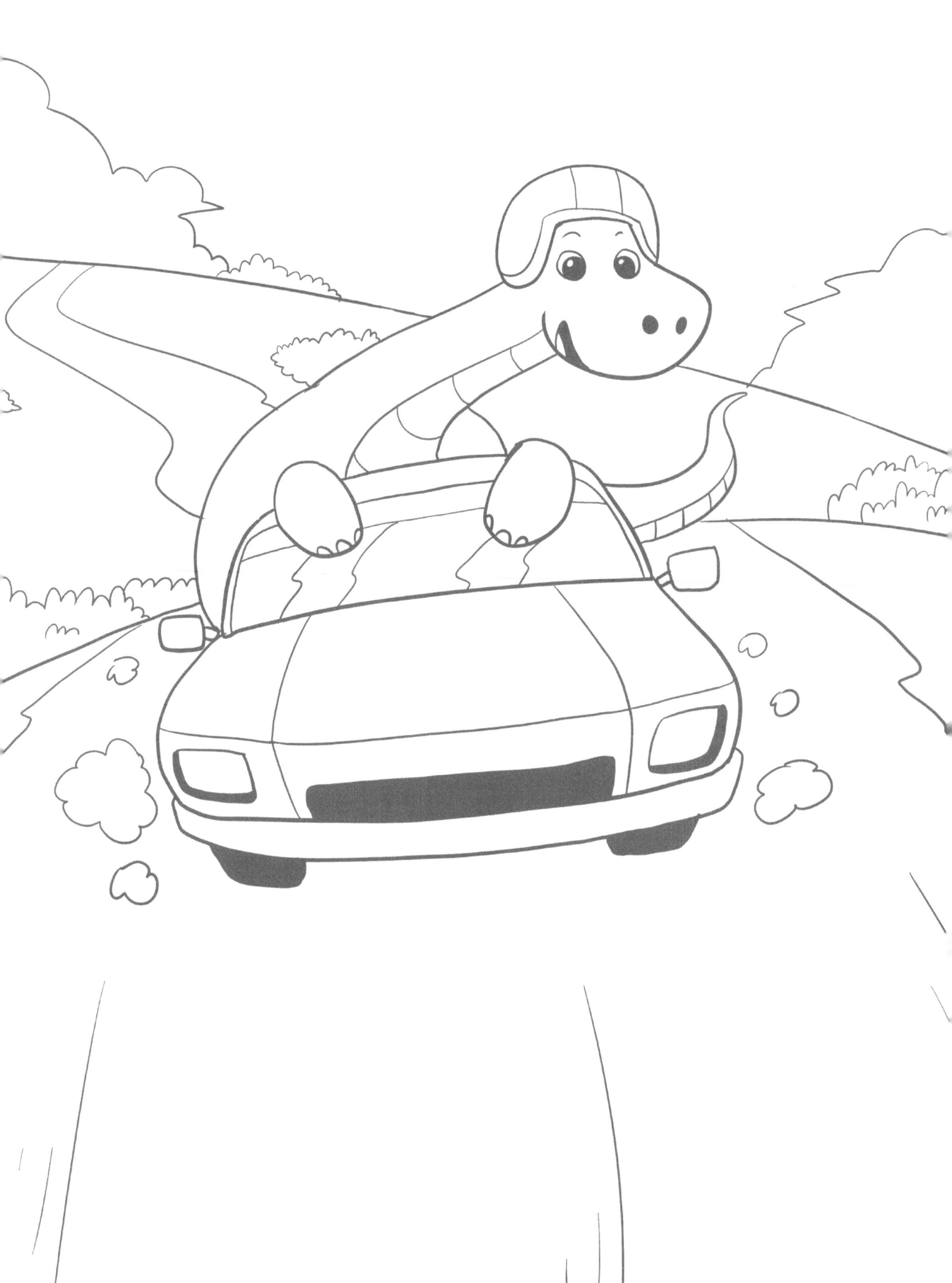

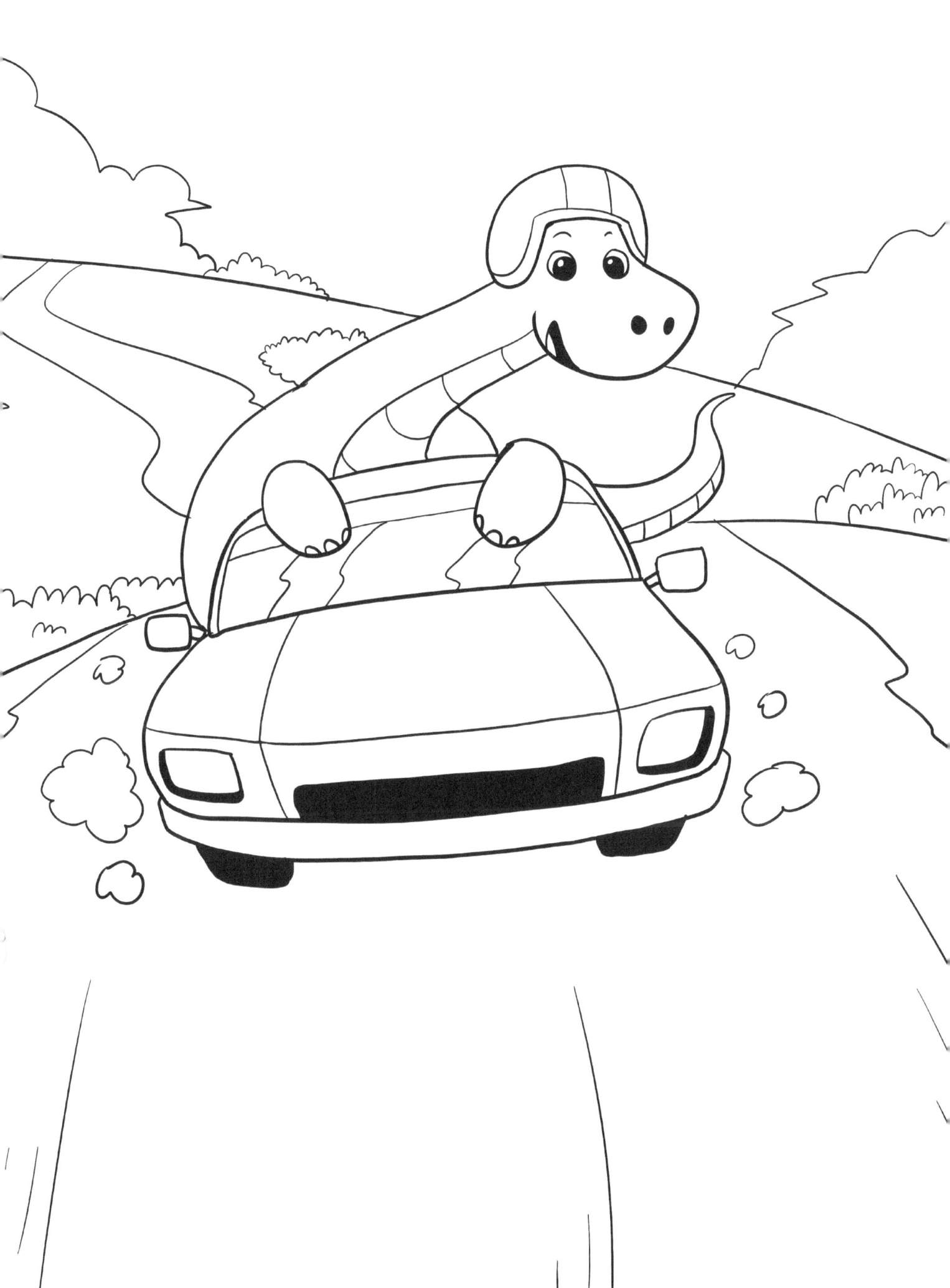

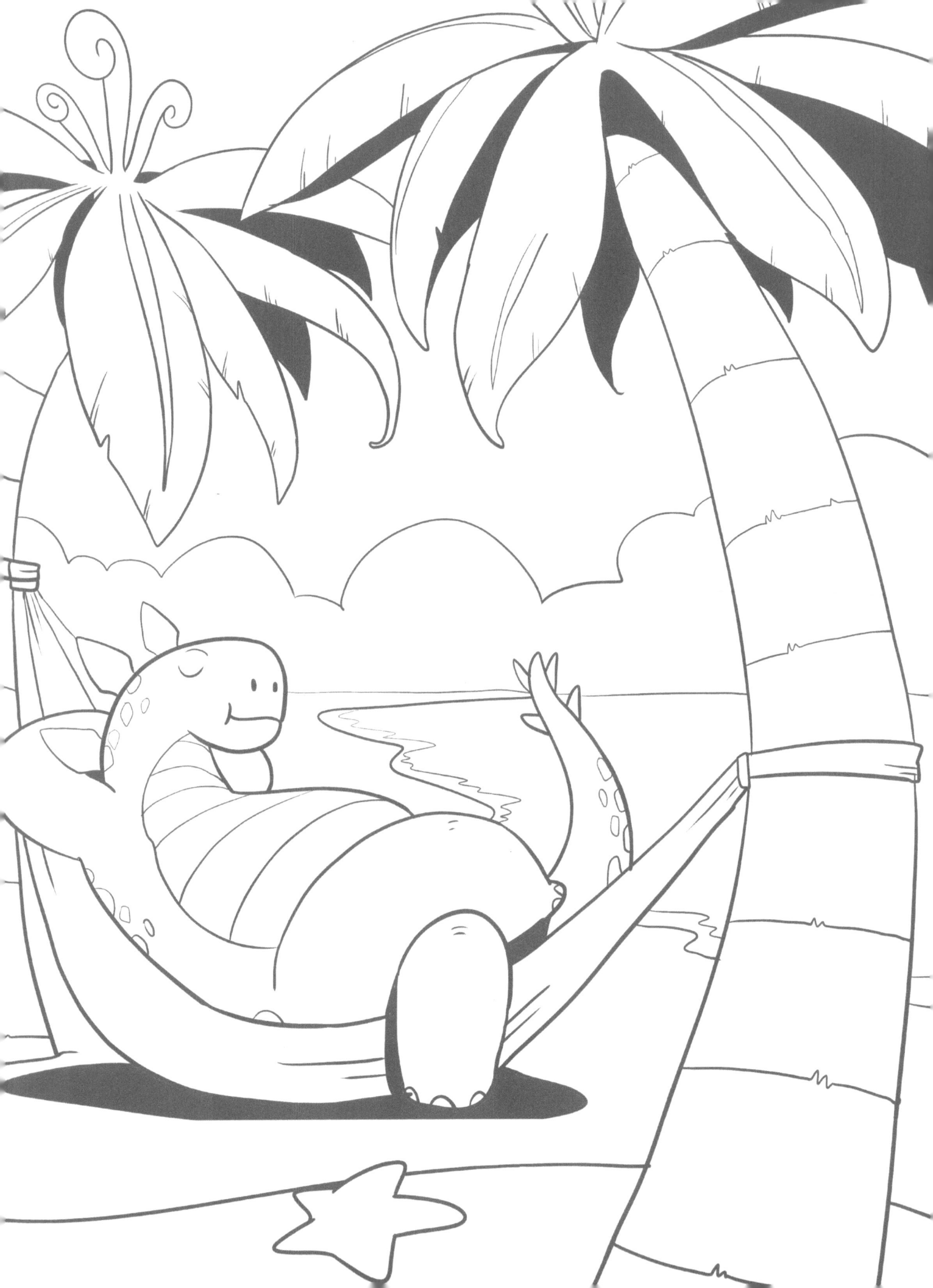

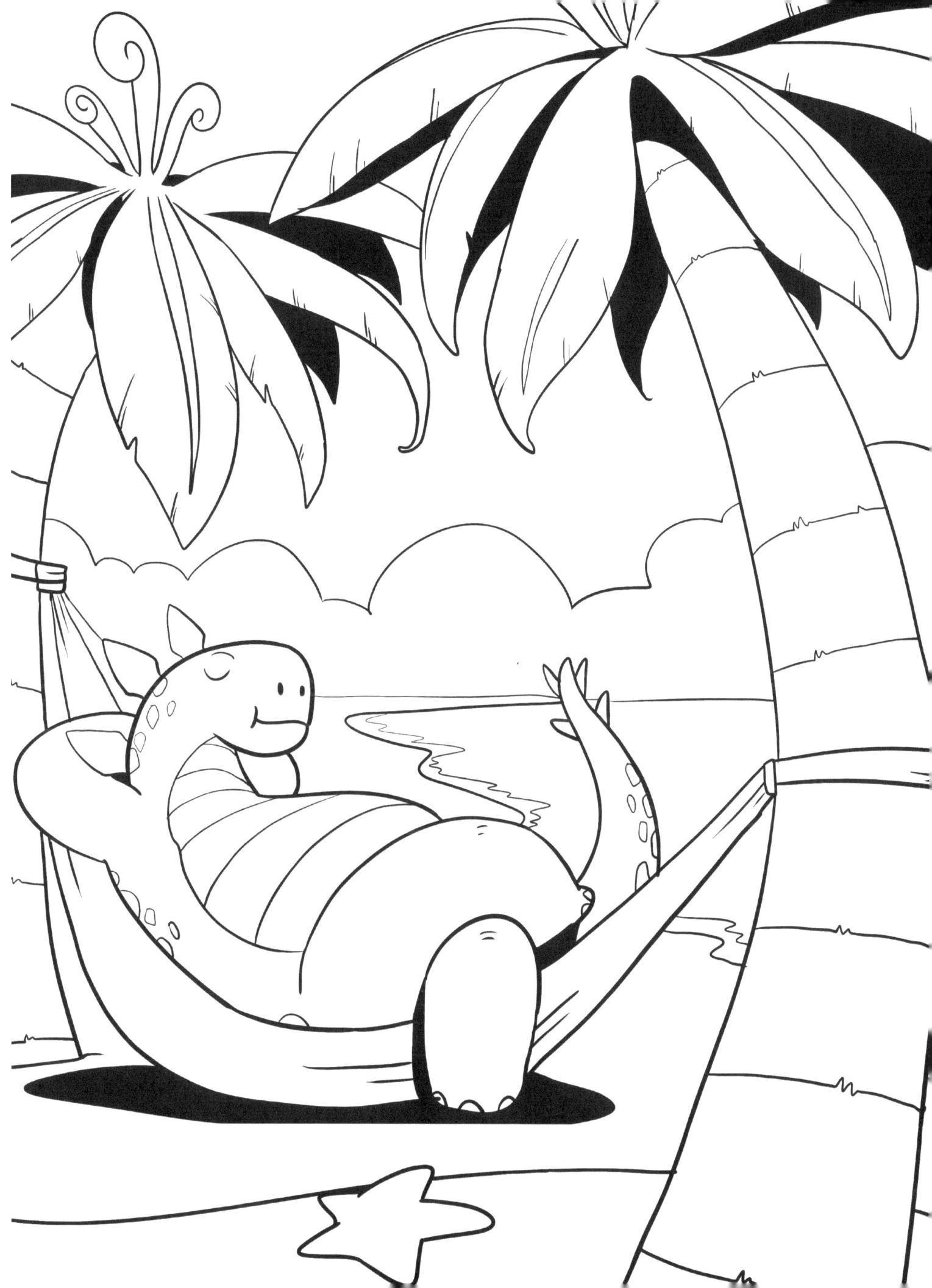

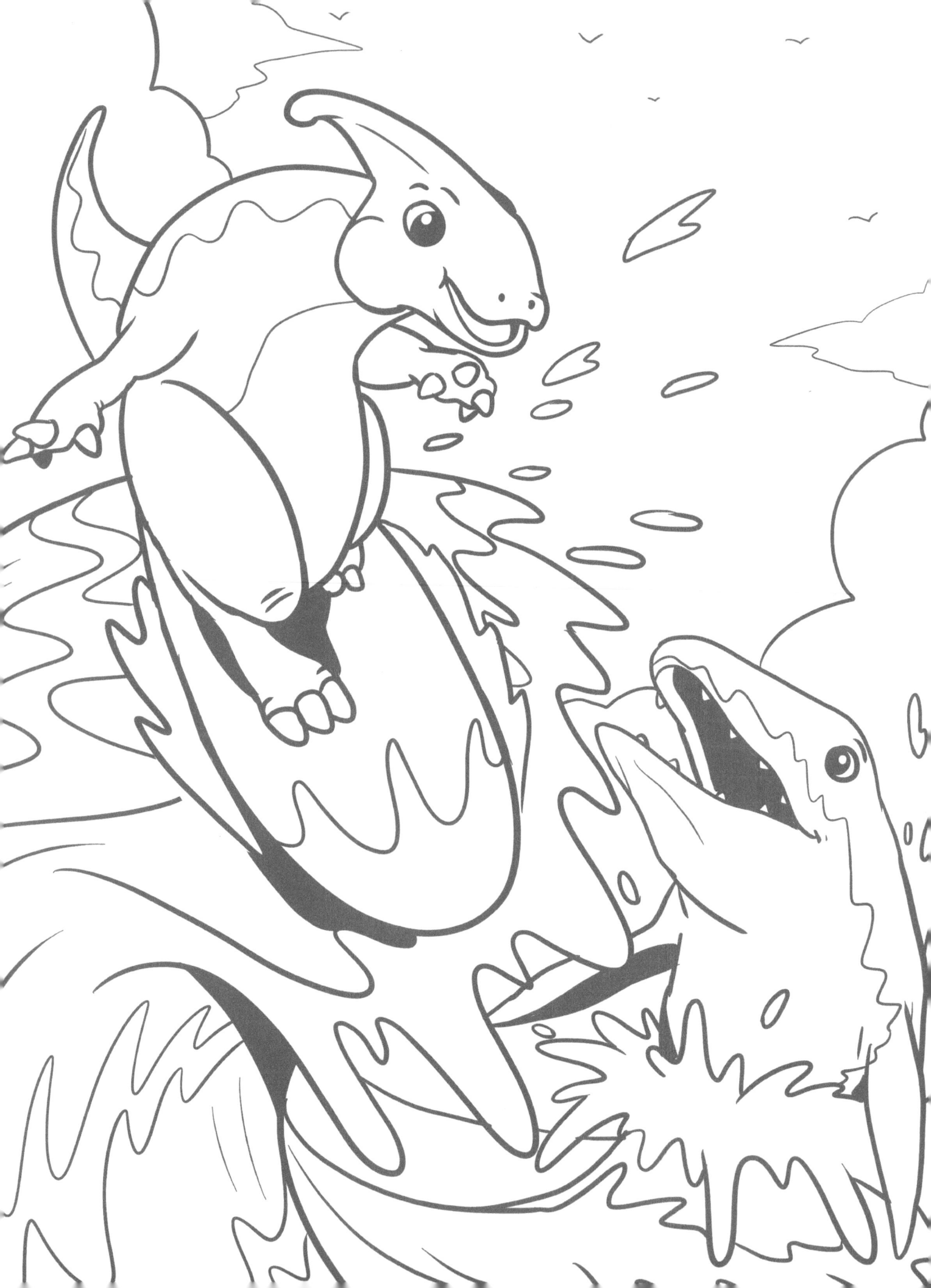

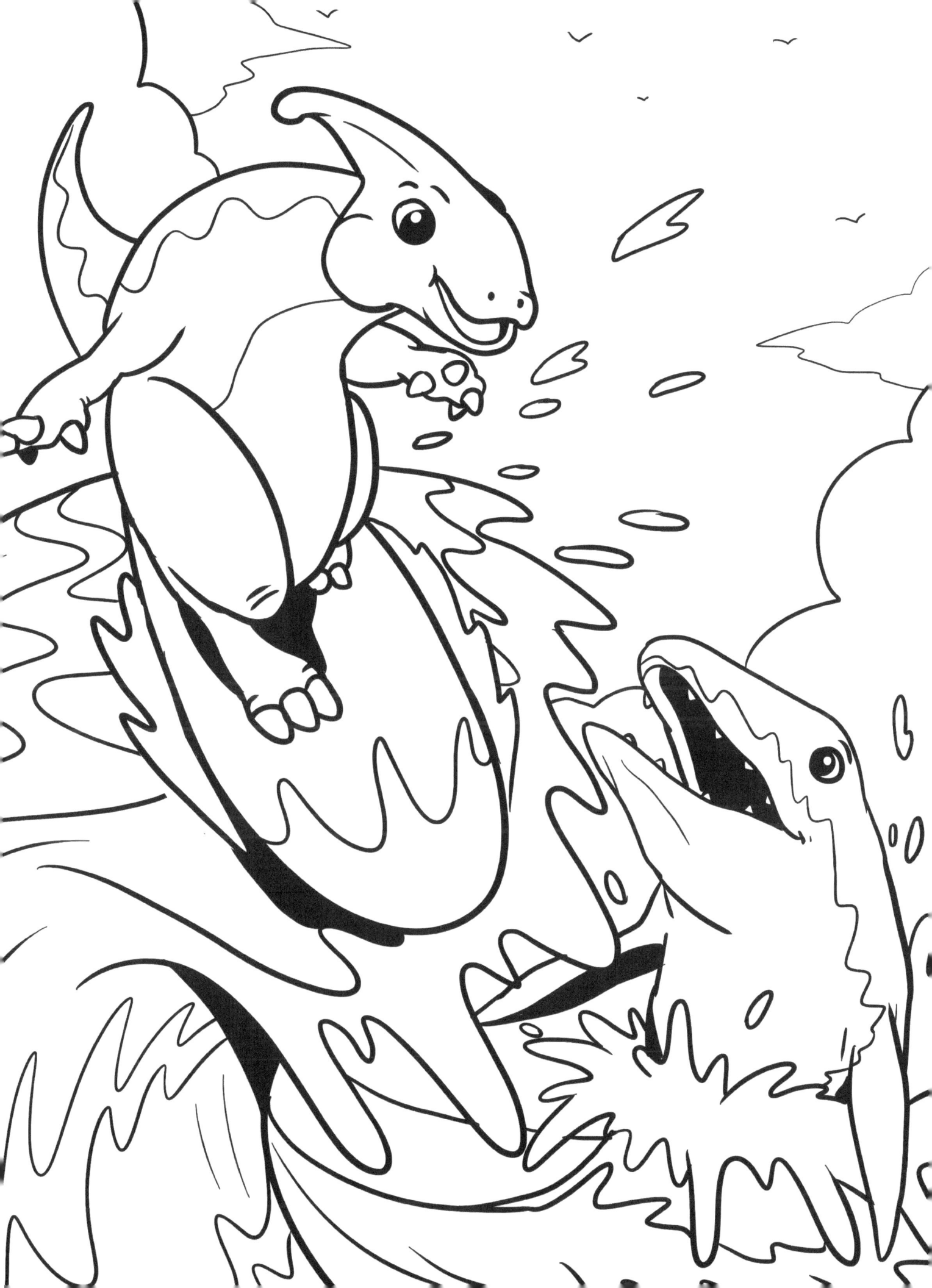

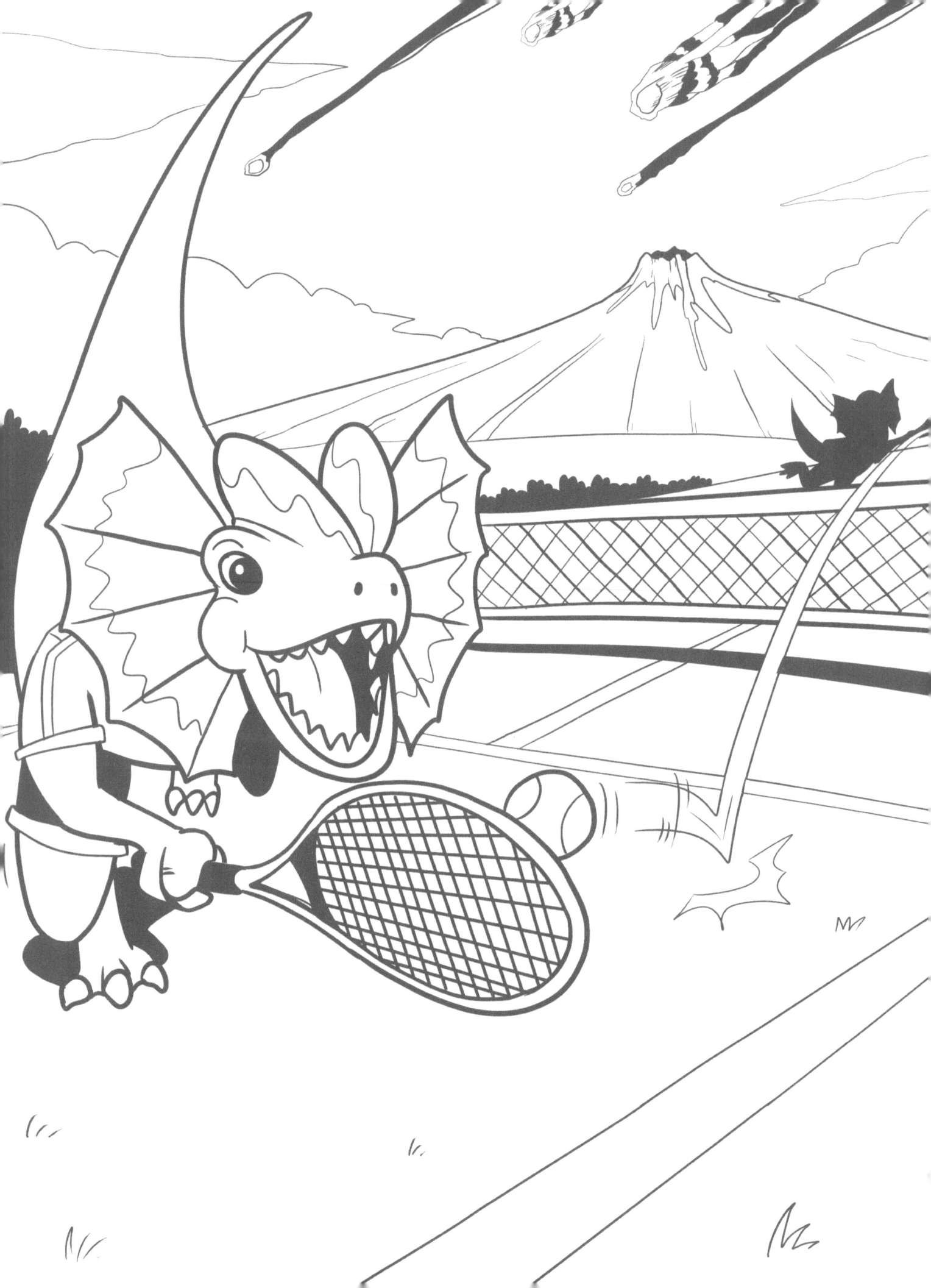

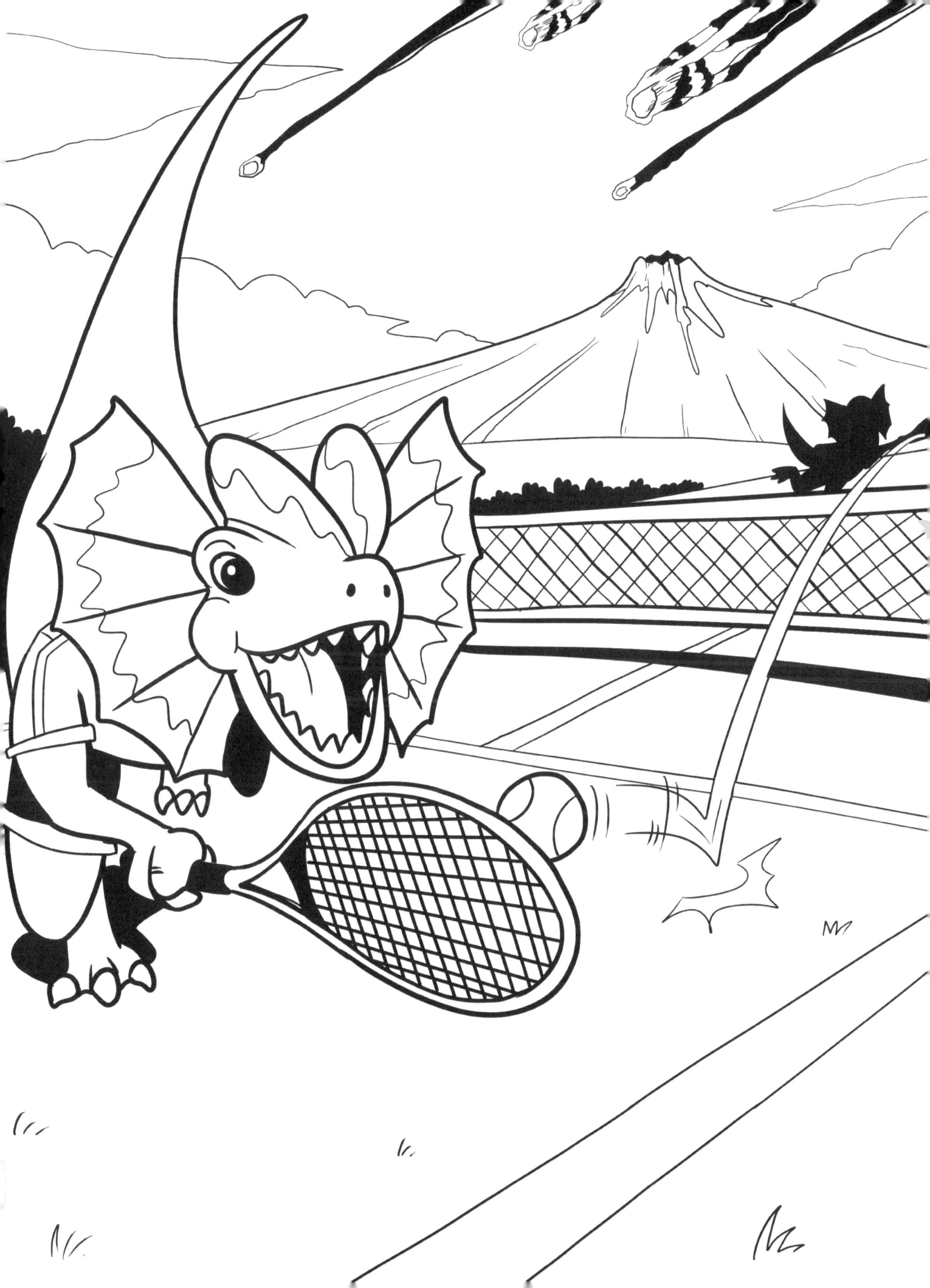

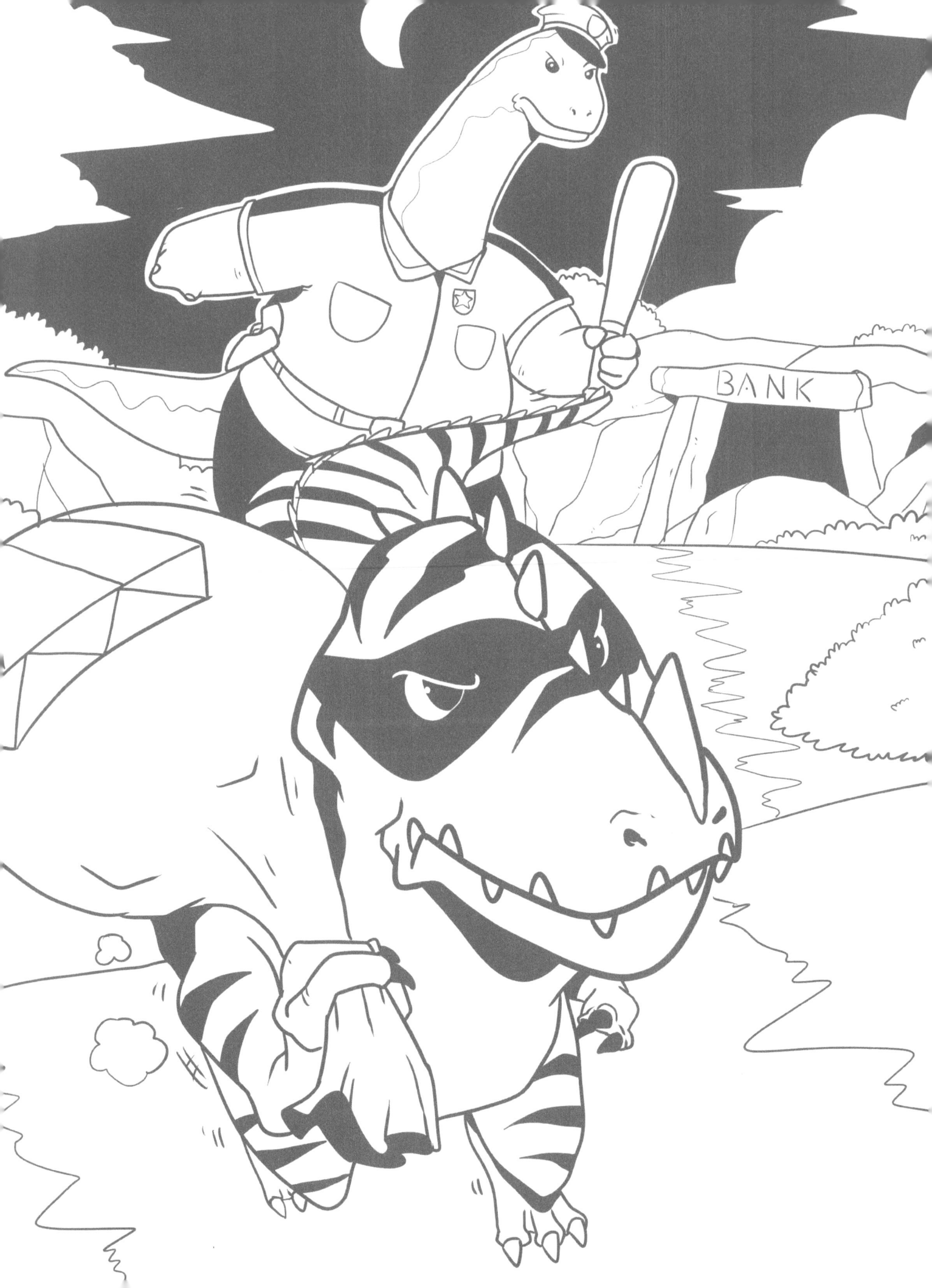

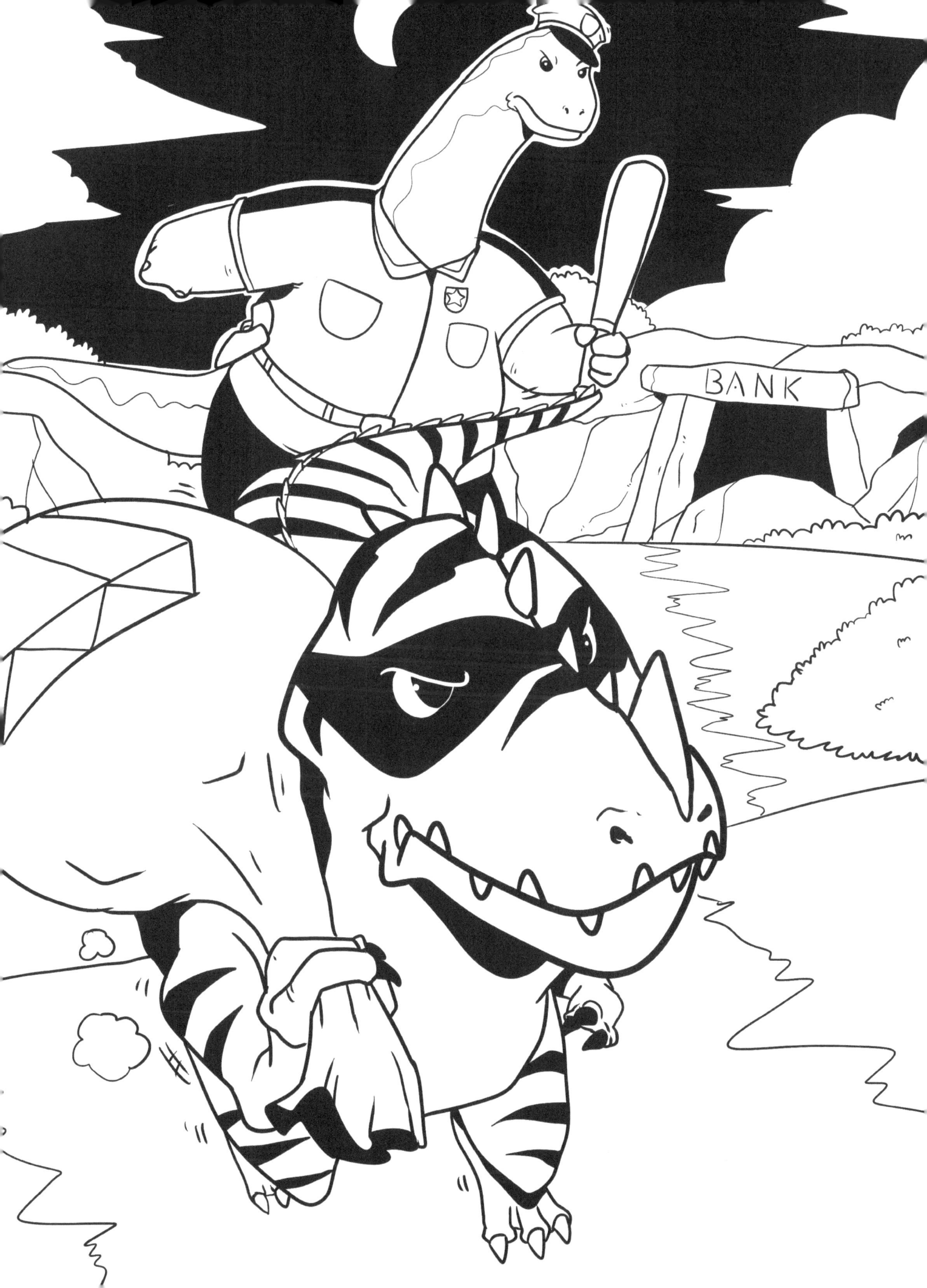

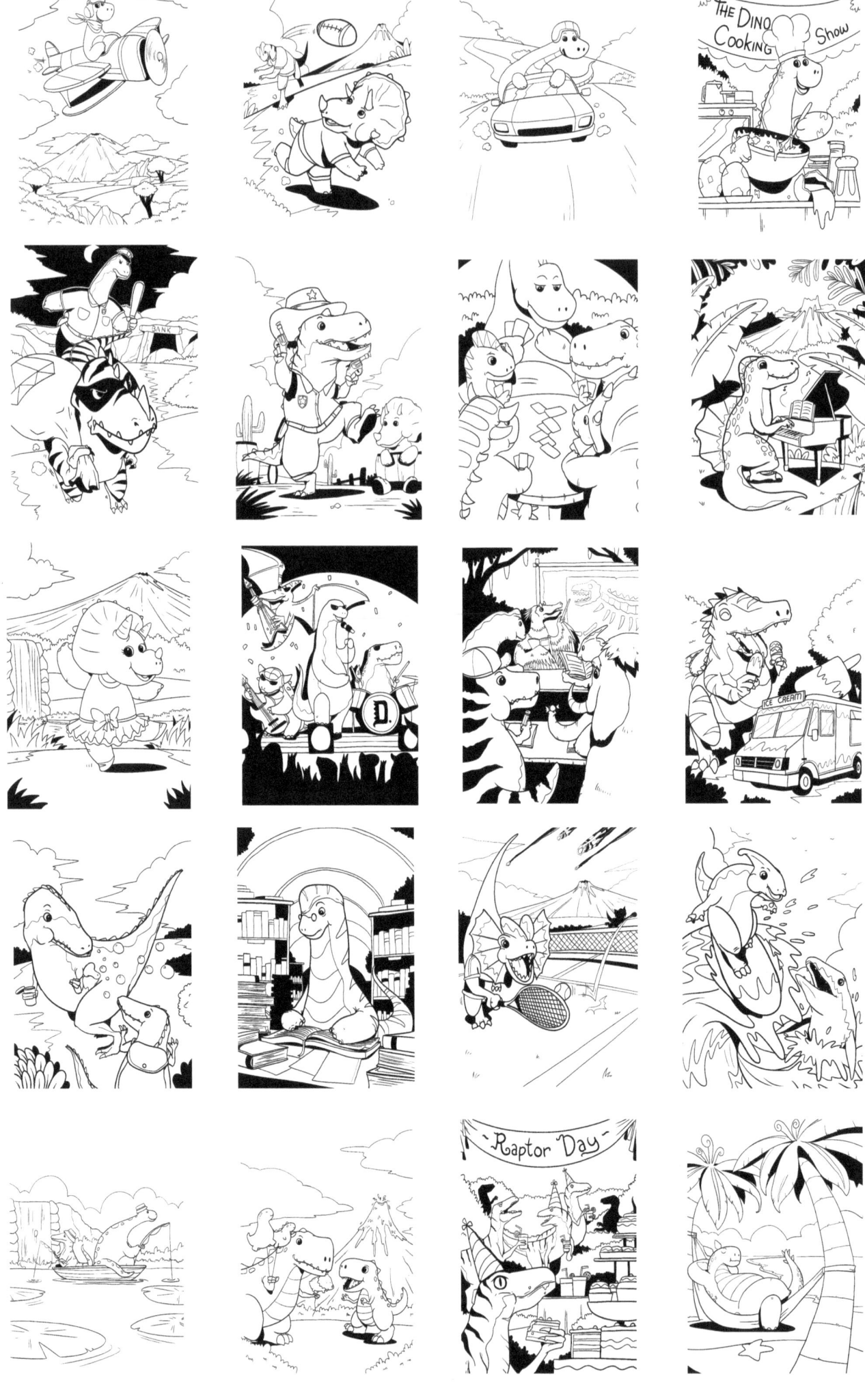

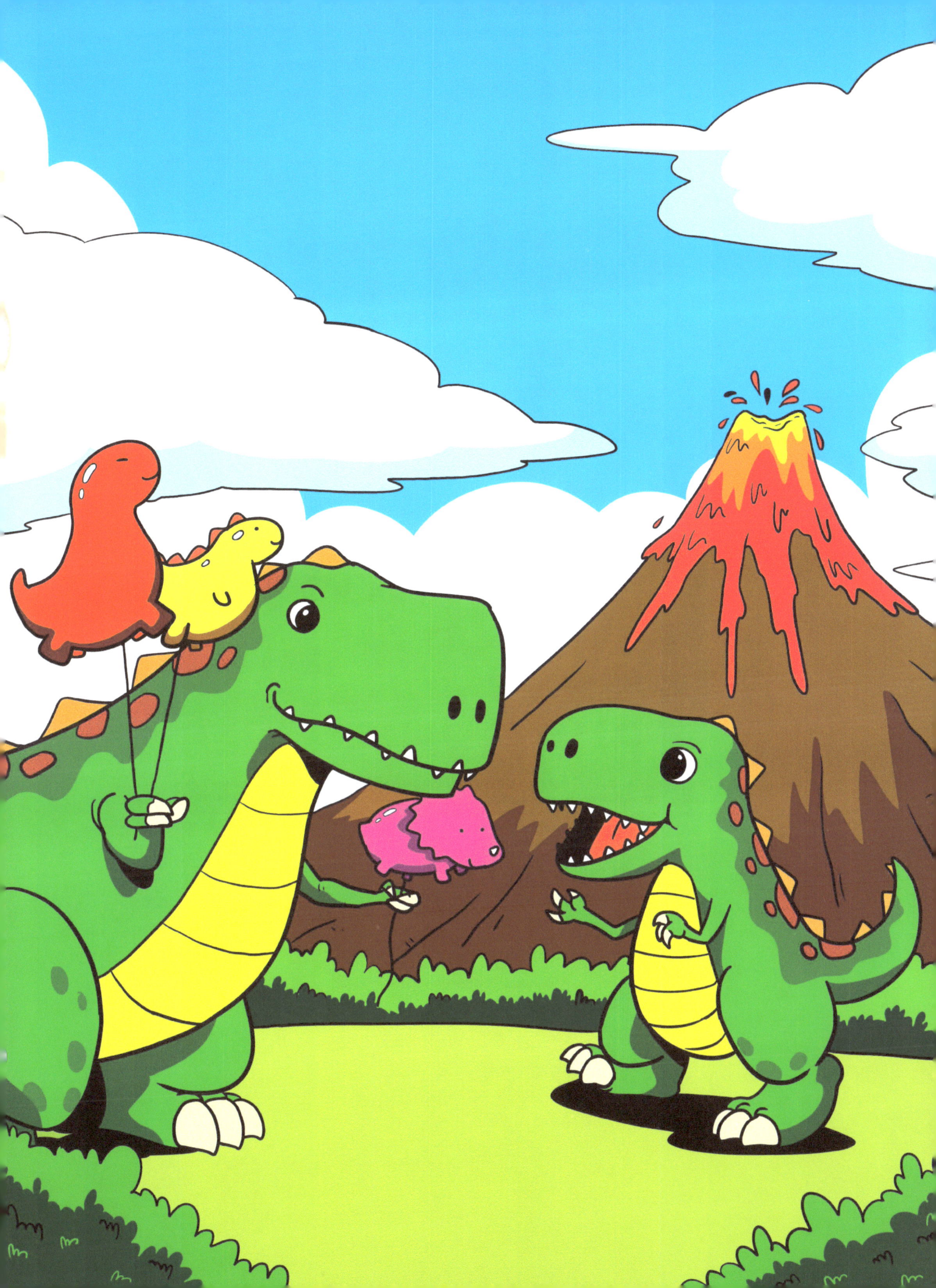

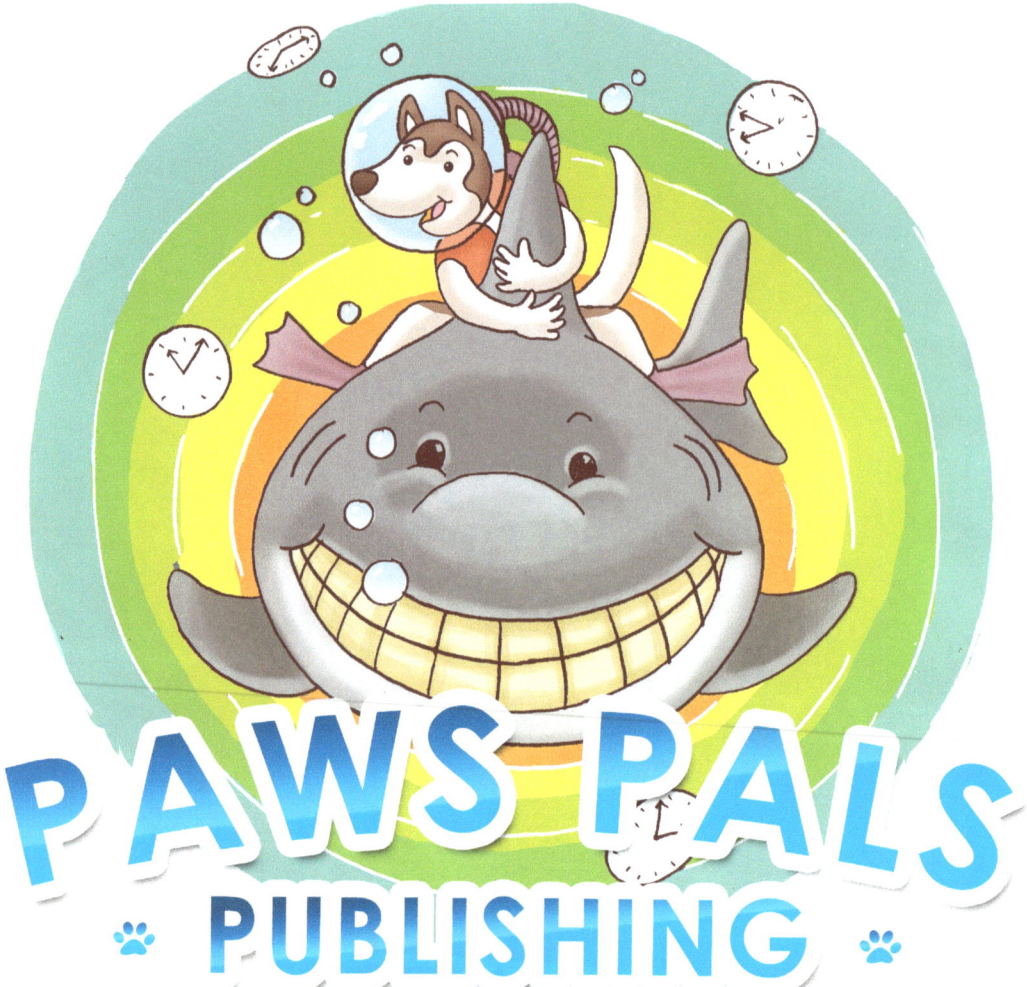

PAWS PALS

PUBLISHING

Published by Andrew Rosenblatt, California April 2016.
www.PawPalsPublishing.com
Library of Congress catalog publication data is available upon request.
ISBN-13: 978-0-9974534-2-3

Printed in America.

First Printed Edition: April 1, 2016.

Created by Andrew Rosenblatt